PEOPLE OF THE SPIRIT

Gifts, Fruit & Fullness of the Holy Spirit

Jack W. Hayford
with
Gary Matsdorf

THOMAS NELSON PUBLISHERS
Nashville

CONTENTS

About the General Editor/About the Writer 4

The Keys That Keep on Freeing 5

Lesson 1:   The Holy Spirit and You 10

Lesson 2:   Holy Spirit Fullness 21

Lesson 3:   The Greatest of These Is Love................... 32

Lesson 4:   Love, Joy, and Peace 43

Lesson 5:   Longsuffering, Kindness, and Goodness........... 53

Lesson 6:   Faithfulness, Gentleness, and Self-Control........... 62

Lesson 7:   Agreeing to Disagree! 71

Lesson 8:   The Creational Gifts............................ 81

Lesson 9:   Office Gifts 95

Lesson 10:   Why All the Fuss?.............................108

Lesson 11:   Word of Wisdom, Word of Knowledge,
             and Faith 118

Lesson 12:   Gifts of Healings, the Working of Miracles,
             and Prophecy.................................130

Lesson 13:   Discerning of Spirits, Different Kinds of Tongues,
             and the Interpretation of Tongues.......................142

People of the Spirit: Gifts, Fruit & Fullness of the Holy Spirit is one of a series of study guides that focus exciting, discovery-geared coverage of Bible book and power themes—all prompting toward dynamic, Holy Spirit-filled living.

About the General Editor

JACK W. HAYFORD, noted pastor, teacher, writer, and composer, is the General Editor of the complete series, working with the publisher in the conceiving and developing of each of the books. Dr. Hayford is Senior Pastor of The Church On The Way, the First Foursquare Church of Van Nuys, California. He and his wife, Anna, have four married children, all of whom are active in either pastoral ministry or vital church life. As General Editor of the *Spirit-Filled Life Bible,* Pastor Hayford led a four-year project, which has resulted in the availability of one of today's most practical and popular study Bibles. He is author of more than twenty books, including *A Passion for Fullness, The Beauty of Spiritual Language, Rebuilding the Real You,* and *Prayer Is Invading the Impossible.* His musical compositions number over four hundred songs, including the widely sung "Majesty."

About the Writer

GARY MATSDORF is pastor of Faith Bible Center in Medford, Oregon, where he has served this growing congregation for more than eleven years. He is a graduate of Azusa Pacific University and Fuller Theological Seminary, and was also a member of the faculty of LIFE Bible College from 1975 to 1981.

Gary and his wife Velda have two children, Travis (15) and Tyler (12). Besides his pastoral duties, Gary is actively involved in missionary work in Jamaica and Spain. He also served as the Associate Editor of the *Spirit-Filled Life Bible.*

Of this contributor, the General Editor has remarked: "Few men have the gift of taking the deeper truths of God's Word and making them both practical and palatable for the average reader/student. Gary's commitment to personal integrity, in scholarship as well as in conduct, brings a unique quality of strength to his writing. I praise God for this kind of edification users of this guide will discover!"

THE KEYS
THAT KEEP ON FREEING

Is there anything that holds more mystery or more genuine practicality than a key? The mystery: "What does it fit? What can it turn on? What might it open? What new discovery could be made? The practicality: Something *will* most certainly open to the possessor! Something *will* absolutely be found to unlock and allow a possibility otherwise obstructed!

- Keys describe the instruments we use to access or ignite.
- Keys describe the concepts that unleash mind-boggling possibilities.
- Keys describe the different structures of musical notes which allow variation and range.

Jesus spoke of keys: "And I will give you the keys of the kingdom of heaven, and whatever you bind on earth will be bound in heaven, and whatever you loose on earth will be loosed in heaven" (Matt. 16:19).

While there is no conclusive list of exactly what keys Jesus was referring to, it is clear that He did confer upon His church—upon *all* who believe—the access to a realm of spiritual partnership with Him in the dominion of His kingdom. Faithful students of the Word of God, moving in the practical grace and biblical wisdom of Holy Spirit-filled living and ministry, have noted some of the primary themes which undergird this order of "spiritual partnership" Christ offers. The "keys" are *concepts*—biblical themes that are traceable through the Scriptures and verifiably dynamic when applied with soundly based faith under the lordship of Jesus Christ. The "partnership" is the *essential* feature of this release of divine grace;

(1) believers reaching to *receive* Christ's promise of "kingdom keys," (2) while choosing to *believe* in the Holy Spirit's readiness to actuate their unleashing, unlimited power today. Companioned with the Bible book studies in the *Spirit-Filled Life Study Guide* series, the Kingdom Dynamic studies present a dozen different themes. This study series is an outgrowth of the Kingdom Dynamics themes included throughout the *Spirit-Filled Life Bible,* which provide a treasury of insight developed by some of today's most respected Christian leaders. From that beginning, studious writers have evolved the elaborated studies you'll pursue here.

The central goal of the subjects focused on in this present series of study guides is to relate "power points" of the Holy Spirit-filled life. Assisting you in your discoveries are a number of helpful features. Each study guide has twelve to fourteen lessons, each arranged so you can plumb the depths or skim the surface, depending upon your needs and interests. The study guides contain major lesson features, each marked by a symbol and heading for easy identification.

 WORD WEALTH

The WORD WEALTH feature provides important definitions of key terms.

 BEHIND THE SCENES

BEHIND THE SCENES supplies information about cultural beliefs and practices, doctrinal disputes, business trades, and the like that illuminate Bible passages and teachings.

AT A GLANCE

The AT A GLANCE feature uses maps and charts to identify places and simplify themes or positions.

 KINGDOM EXTRA

Because this study guide focuses on a theme of the Bible, you will find a KINGDOM EXTRA feature that guides you into Bible dictionaries, Bible encyclopedias, and other resources that will enable you to glean more from the Bible's wealth on the topic if you want something extra.

 PROBING THE DEPTHS

Another feature, PROBING THE DEPTHS, will explain controversial issues raised by particular lessons and cite Bible passages and other sources to which you can turn to help you come to your own conclusions.

 FAITH ALIVE

Finally, each lesson contains a FAITH ALIVE feature. Here the focus is, So what? Given what the Bible says, what does it mean for my life? How can it impact my day-to-day needs, hurts, relationships, concerns, and whatever else is important to me? FAITH ALIVE will help you see and apply the practical relevance of God's literary gift.

As you'll see, these guides supply space for you to answer the study and life-application questions and exercises. You may, however, want to record all your answers, or just the overflow from your study or application, in a separate notebook or journal. This would be especially helpful if you think you'll dig into the KINGDOM EXTRA features. Because the exercises in this feature are optional and can be expanded as far as you want to take them, we have not allowed writing space for them in this study guide. So you may want to have a notebook or journal handy for recording your discoveries while working through to this feature's riches.

The Bible study method used in this series revolves around four basic steps: observation, interpretation, correlation, and application. Observation answers the question, What does the text say? Interpretation deals with, What does the text mean?—not with what it means to you or me, but what it meant to its original readers. Correlation asks, What light do other Scripture passages shed on this text? And application, the goal of Bible study, poses the question, How should my life change in response to the Holy Spirit's teaching of this text?

If you have used a Bible much before, you know that it comes in a variety of translations and paraphrases. Although you can use any of them with profit as you work through the *Spirit-Filled Life Kingdom Dynamics Study Guide* series, when Bible passages or words are cited, you will find they are from the New King James Version of the Bible. Using this translation with this series will make your study easier, but it's certainly not necessary.

The only resources you need to complete and apply these study guides are a heart and mind open to the Holy Spirit, a prayerful attitude, and a pencil and a Bible. Of course, you may draw upon other sources, such as commentaries, dictionaries, encyclopedias, atlases, and concordances, and you'll even find some optional exercises that will guide you into these sources. But these are extras, not necessities. These study guides are comprehensive enough to give you all you need to gain a good, basic understanding of the Bible book being covered and how you can apply its themes and counsel to your life.

A word of warning, though. By itself, Bible study will not transform your life. It will not give you power, peace, joy, comfort, hope, and a number of other gifts God longs for you to unwrap and enjoy. Through Bible study, you will grow in your understanding of the Lord, His kingdom and your place in it, and those things are essential. But you need more. You need to rely on the Holy Spirit to guide your study and your application of the Bible's truths. He, Jesus promised, was sent to teach us "all things" (John 14:26; cf. 1 Cor. 2:13). So as you use this series to guide you through Scripture, bathe your study time in prayer, asking the Spirit of God to illuminate the text, enlighten your mind, humble your will, and comfort your heart. He will never let you down.

My prayer and goal for you is that as you unlock and begin to explore God's Book for living His way, the Holy Spirit will fill every fiber of your being with the joy and power God longs to give all His children. So read on. Be diligent. Stay open and submissive to Him. You will not be disappointed. He promises you!

Lesson 1/ The Holy Spirit and You

Say "spirit" and no doubt varied images come to people's minds. For some "spirit" is synonymous with haunted mansions and "ghosts"; for others it refers to some sort of cosmic life force. To those committed to biblical truth, "spirit" denotes either (1) unclean, demonic forces (Matt. 12:43); (2) that part of man with which God most intimately communicates (Rom. 8:16); or (3) the Holy Spirit, third Person of the Trinity—the very Spirit of God (Matt. 12:28) and of Jesus Christ (2 Cor. 3:17)—who is seen in the Bible primarily as carrying out the ministries of the Father and the Son.

The importance of the Spirit in Jesus' life is noted by the fact that Jesus begins His public ministry with the reception of the Spirit (Matt. 3:13–17). Luke describes Jesus as "being filled with the Holy Spirit" (4:1) and as ministering "in the power of the Spirit" (4:14). Jesus Himself attributes the dynamism of His ministry to the Holy Spirit (Matt. 12:28), a dynamism which He passes on directly to His leading disciples by breathing on them and saying, "Receive the Holy Spirit" (John 20:22). This is but the beginning of what John the Baptist prophesied when he said that Jesus would "baptize . . . with the Holy Spirit" (Mark 1:8).

Who is this Person who empowered Jesus and was passed on to His followers? What are His specific attributes? Why did Jesus term Him "another" Helper (John 14:16)? What is His personal relationship to believers? Our first lesson will explore the Person of the Holy Spirit and our personal relationship to Him. It will also help clarify some often misunderstood biblical terminology about Holy Spirit baptism which will set the pace for the remainder of our study. Let's explore together!

THE PERSON OF THE HOLY SPIRIT

Read the following scriptures and record what you observe about the Holy Spirit.

What does the Bible say about the Spirit as an intelligent Person?

John 15:26

John 16:13

Acts 13:2

Does He demonstrate emotion and exercise will?

Rom. 15:30

1 Cor. 12:11

1 Thess. 5:19

Are there attributes of deity assigned to Him?

Acts 5:3, 4

1 Cor. 2:10

Heb. 9:14

What are some of His specific New Testament names?

John 14:17

Rom. 8:9

1 Cor. 3:16

Phil. 1:19

What are some New Testament symbols ascribed to Him?

Matt. 3:16

John 3:8

John 7:37–39

We see then that the Holy Spirit is not a force—He's a Person. He is intelligent and exercises emotion and will. He is equated with God Himself (Acts 5:3, 4) and knows the Father's very depths. No wonder the church continues to sing, "Praise Father, Son, and Holy Ghost"!

CHRISTMAS, EASTER, AND THE HOLY SPIRIT

Christmas and Easter—the two formidable events that underlie Christianity. The marvel of God become flesh was matched only by the marvel of Jesus Christ's sacrificial death and triumphant resurrection. Sent by the love of the Father (John 3:16) and "raised from the dead by [His] glory" (Rom. 6:4), the Son "made Himself of no reputation, taking the form of a bondservant, *and* coming in the likeness of men . . . to *the point of* death, even the death of the cross" (Phil. 2:7, 8). And what about the Holy Spirit? Read the following and note His direct involvement in both the Christmas and Easter events.

Matt. 1:18–20

Luke 1:13–15

Luke 1:41

Luke 1:67

Luke 2:25–27

Rom. 1:4

Rom. 8:11

 **WORD WEALTH**

Spirit, *pneuma.* Compare "pneumonia," "pneumatology," "pneumatic." Breath, breeze, a current of air, wind, spirit.

Pneuma is that part of a person capable of responding to God. The Holy Spirit is the third person of the Trinity, who draws us to Christ, convicts us of sin, enables us to accept Christ as our personal Savior, assures us of salvation, enables us to live the victorious life, understand the Bible, pray according to God's will, and share Christ with others.[1]

 ### BEHIND THE SCENES

One of the distinctives of the Christian faith is the doctrine of the Trinity, the Father, the Son, and the Holy Spirit coexisting in the unity of the Godhead. Although the word *Trinity* is not found in the Bible, the concept is clearly taught. The Trinity is specifically acknowledged by Jesus in His baptismal statement in the Great Commission (Matt. 28:19) and in Paul's benediction to the Corinthians (2 Cor. 13:14). Confession of belief in the Trinity appears in the Nicene Creed (A.D. 381) and the Roman Symbol, a brief creedal statement from at least as far back as the fourth century. The famous Apostles' Creed, formalized in the sixth century and forming the basis for much of evangelical Christianity's doctrine, states specifically, "I believe in God the Father Almighty . . . and in Jesus Christ His Son . . . and in the Holy Spirit."

THE ONENESS OF GOD

What do the following scriptures teach us about the fundamental oneness or unity of God?

Mark 12:29

John 17:3

1 Cor. 8:6

EXISTING IN THREE PERSONS

What do the following scriptures teach us about that which Calvin terms "a more intimate knowledge of His nature"?

Mark 1:10, 11

1 Cor. 12:4–6

2 Cor. 13:14

JESUS' CONCERN

Just prior to His crucifixion, Jesus had a tremendous concern for the welfare of His disciples and future church. "Let not your heart be troubled" (John 14:1) were His words of comfort, followed by the promise that He would "pray the Father, and He will give you another Helper, that He may abide with you forever" (v. 16).

The preciousness of this promise comes home as we understand the meaning of the Greek word translated "another."

WORD WEALTH

Another, *allos.* One besides, another of the same kind. The word shows similarities but diversities of operation and ministries. Jesus' use of *allos* for sending another Comforter equals "one besides Me and in addition to Me but one just like Me. He will do in My absence what I would do if I were physically present with you." The Spirit's coming assures continuity with what Jesus did and taught.² "Continuity of what Jesus did and taught!" No wonder Luke presents Acts as a continuation through Holy Spirit fullness "of all that Jesus began both to do and teach" (1:1). Jesus goes on in John 14 to state some more valuable insights about the Holy Spirit which prove very helpful to gaining a fuller understanding of who He is. Let's follow Him.

He's the Spirit of _____ (v. 17).

His relationship to believers is that of dwelling _____ us (v. 17).

He's our _____ (v. 26).

He will _____ us all things (v. 26).

    WORD WEALTH

Helper, *parakletos.* From *para,* "beside," and *kaleo,* "to call," hence, called to one's side. The word signifies an intercessor, comforter, helper, advocate, counselor. In nonbiblical literature *parakletos* had the technical meaning of an attorney who appears in court in another's behalf. The Holy Spirit leads believers to a greater apprehension of gospel truths. In addition to general help and guidance, He gives the strength to endure the hostility of the world system.³

AT A GLANCE

THE WORK OF THE HOLY SPIRIT (Acts 2:4)[4]
In the beginning • Active and present at creation, hovering over the unordered conditions (Gen. 1:2)
In the Old Testament • The origin of supernatural abilities (Gen. 41:38) • The giver of artistic skill (Ex. 31:2–5) • The source of power and strength (Judg. 3:9, 10) • The inspiration of prophecy (1 Sam. 19:20, 23) • The mediation of God's message (Mic. 3:8)
In Old Testament prophecy • The cleansing of the heart for holy living (Ezek. 36:25–29)
In salvation • Brings conviction (John 16:8–11) • Regenerates the believer (Titus 3:5) • Sanctifies the believer (2 Thess. 2:13) • Completely indwells the believer (John 14:17; Rom. 8:9–11)
In the New Testament • Imparts spiritual truth (John 14:26; 16:13; 1 Cor. 2:13–15) • Glorifies Christ (John 16:14) • Endows with power for gospel proclamation (Acts 1:8) • Fills believers (Acts 2:4) • Pours out God's love in the heart (Rom. 5:5) • Enables believers to walk in holiness (Rom. 8:1–8; Gal. 5:16–25) • Makes intercession (Rom. 8:26) • Imparts gifts for ministry (1 Cor. 12:4–11) • Strengthens the inner being (Eph. 3:16)
In the written Word • Inspired the writing of Scripture (2 Tim. 3:16; 2 Pet. 1:21)

> The New Testament understands the Holy Spirit to be the assurance of the risen Lord Jesus indwelling believers.

STOP . . . BEFORE PROCEEDING!

A passion for the Spirit's fullness can cause us to forget He is a Person—not a force. We must not let this happen. As the third Person of the Godhead, the Spirit must always retain His rightful position as intelligent, emotive deity.

THE SPIRIT'S PERSONAL RELATIONSHIP TO YOU

Are you now convinced more than ever that the Holy Spirit is a wonderful Person? Hopefully so. But where do we as Christians stand with relationship to Him? Before probing His fullness in our lives, we need to understand His fundamental relationship with us. What happens between the Holy Spirit and a person at the moment of conversion? Again let's explore.

According to Jesus, how does one meet the Holy Spirit?(John 3:5)

What does Paul say about every Christian and the Holy Spirit? (Rom. 8:9)

How does 1 Corinthians 12:13 describe this *initial*, fundamental encounter with the Spirit?

 PROBING THE DEPTHS

In 1 Corinthians 12:13 Paul writes, "By one Spirit we were all baptized into one body." Regarding this verse Don Pickerill writes, "The Greek grammar in this statement parallels other passages that speak of being 'baptized with the Holy Spirit' (see Matt. 3:11; Mark 1:8; Luke 3:16; John 1:33; Acts 1:5; 11:16). While Spirit baptism describes a primary spiritual reality for all believers, Paul still pleads for a Spirit-filled experience (Eph. 5:18) that includes the manifestations" listed in 1 Corinthians 12:8–11.[5]

In other words, in its most basic form Holy Spirit baptism means to be converted, to be placed into the body of Christ.

"It should be understood that by 'baptism in the Holy Spirit' the traditional Pentecostal/Charismatic does not refer to that baptism *of* the Holy Spirit accomplished at conversion, whereby the believer is placed *into* the body of Christ by faith in His redeeming work on the Cross."[6] Read the following verses for yourself, noting what each says about this:

Rom. 6:3, 4

1 Cor. 12:13

Gal. 3:26, 27

HOLY SPIRIT, WORK IN MY LIFE

Although our entire study deals with the work of the Holy Spirit in our lives, there are some fundamental works we need to highlight before proceeding.

What is one of the Spirit's primary works in the life of a Christian? (Rom. 8:16; Gal. 4:6)

What is another primary work of the Spirit in the life of a Christian? (Eph. 1:13, 14)

What does 1 Corinthians 2:12 state about receiving the Spirit and understanding spiritual gifts?

What is the Spirit's role in the strengthening of our inner man? (Eph. 3:16)

Ephesians 3:16 notes that the Spirit is the One who mediates power in the life of the believer. Spirit and power are often linked in Paul's writing. Read the following texts and note what He associates with "the Spirit and power."

1 Cor. 2:4

1 Thess. 1:5

 FAITH ALIVE

What have you learned here that is new to you? What have you had refocused? Can you clearly see that all Christians, including yourself, have the Spirit personally? How should this affect the way you might ask other Christians whether or not they "have the Spirit" or even whether or not they have been "baptized with the Spirit"?

How about beginning now by thanking God for the Holy Spirit in your life? He is a precious Gift who has brought us salvation; as such, we need to express appreciation for this initial baptism before seeking a fuller baptism from Him.

1. *Spirit-Filled Life Bible* (Nashville, TN: Thomas Nelson Publishers, 1991), 1697, "Word Wealth: 7:6 Spirit."
2. Ibid., 1603, "Word Wealth: 14:16 another."
3. Ibid., 1605, "Word Wealth: 15:26 Helper."
4. Ibid., 1626, "Chart: The Work of the Holy Spirit (Acts 2:4)."
5. Ibid., 1737, note on 12:13.
6. Ibid., 2020, "Holy Spirit Gifts and Power."

Lesson 2/Holy Spirit Fullness

Have you ever turned up the flame of a gas burner and watched boiling water respond? The higher the flame, the faster the boil. Right? Though somewhat of an inadequate analogy, this does serve to explain in part the relational dynamic between the Holy Spirit and Christians. As established in the first lesson, all "born again" people have the indwelling Holy Spirit (Rom. 8:9). It is He "who is the guarantee of our inheritance until the redemption of the purchased possession" (Eph. 1:14). But this is only the beginning! He is a dynamic Person who desires a dynamic—not a static—relationship with His people. Why leave Him then as a mere "pilot light" in our lives when He can fully impassion us with God's fruitful life and dynamic gifts? We are to be "fervent [*zeo,* "fiery hot," "full of burning zeal"] in spirit" (Rom. 12:11).

How does all this fullness become part of us? Is there a definite starting point following our initial salvation? Can we have a one-time experience with the Holy Spirit that lasts forever, or is fullness to be sought daily? How can we know if we're aglow with the Spirit? These are some of the pertinent questions which this study will seek to answer. But be warned—it will take some thinking! We'll need to grapple with a lot of scriptures and with various terms; is "being filled with the Spirit" the same as "having Him poured out in our lives"? the same as "being baptized with the Holy Spirit"? Furthermore, we'll need to realize that when all is said and done, we might have some answers not acceptable to some segments of conservative Christianity! This does not mean our perspective is "superior" and theirs "inferior." It simply means that the fullness of the Spirit is one of those doctrines (like the timing of Jesus' return) which can be interpreted with diversity.

Therefore, not all evangelical Christians agree with each other! (Won't it be wonderful when we no longer "see in a mirror, dimly" [1 Cor. 13:12], and all our doctrinal differences are resolved around the throne of grace?)

ABUNDANCE OR TRICKLE?

Let's take a look at God's view on His giving of the Holy Spirit to us. Experience shows that if we are going to seek after something, we need to know what it is we're seeking, and we need to be convinced of its importance. Therefore, if we're going to see the fullness of the Spirit in our lives, we need to understand how important that fullness is to God, the Giver. Let's see what the New Testament says about God's perspective. We'll start with His giving of the Spirit to Jesus Christ Himself and then move on to His giving the Spirit to us.

Looking to Jesus as a Model, how does Luke describe the Spirit at work in His life? (Luke 4:1)

What does John 3:34 say about God's giving of the Spirit to Jesus?

According to Luke 4:18, 19, what were the fundamental purposes of the Spirit's coming upon Jesus?

In his Pentecost sermon (Acts 2:14–36), Peter gives us God's perspective on how He intends to give His Spirit to the church. He does so by quoting the Old Testament prophet Joel. According to verse 17, God's intent is to _____ of His Spirit on all flesh.

How is this same dynamic outpouring described in John 7:38, 39?

Commenting on this Johannine passage Siegfried Schatzmann notes, "Those who are satisfied by Jesus will themselves become channels of spiritual refreshment for others. The figure of rivers contrasts with 'a fountain' (4:14), illustrating the difference between one's new birth and one's experience of the overflowing fullness of the Spirit-filled life."[1]

When Peter testifies before the religious ruling body of Jerusalem, what does Luke specifically note about his relationship to the Holy Spirit? (Acts 4:8)

What does Luke note about Paul and the Holy Spirit when Paul confronts the magician Bar-Jesus? (Acts 13:9)

What can we conclude so far then about the relationship God desires all Christians to have with His Holy Spirit?

In light of this, what does Ephesians 5:18 command of us?

 BEHIND THE SCENES

In Ephesians 5:18, "dissipation" translates the Greek word *asotia,* meaning sexual excess and debauchery. Its related verb describes the prodigal son who "wasted his possessions with <u>prodigal</u> living" (Luke 15:13). Dissipation is the epitome of folly; Spirit-filled living stands in contrast, then, as the epitome of wisdom.

"The tense of the Greek for 'be filled' makes clear that such a Spirit-filled condition does not stop with a single experience, but is maintained by 'continually being filled,' as commanded here."[2] Such continuous fillings, as exampled above in Peter before the Sanhedrin, are necessary if we are to live wise lives of worship (Eph. 5:15–21).

 PROBING THE DEPTHS

Carefully reread Ephesians 5:15–21. Make a list of the benefits/results Paul associates with being continuously Spirit- filled.

TERMS, TERMS AND MORE TERMS!

A major key to understanding the New Testament's teachings on the fullness of the Holy Spirit in our lives is to realize that our relationship with Him is described using several different phrases—all basically meaning the same thing! It's what is known as "fluid language"—the terms change, but not the concept. Jesus Himself used "fluid language" by sometimes referring to His divine reign as "the kingdom of God" while at other times calling it "the kingdom of heaven." On one occasion He used both terms in a single breath (Matt. 19:23, 24)! With this understanding, let's do some exploring in Acts.

Luke begins by quoting Jesus as saying the Holy Spirit shall "come upon you" (1:8). What terminology does Luke then use to define the most immediate fulfillment of this promise? (2:4)

How does Luke term this same relational dynamic to the Holy Spirit in these verses?

8:17

9:17

10:44

10:45

19:6

Does it not seem to you, therefore, that Luke's concern is more in conveying a relational dynamic than in giving a tightly worded theology? This in no way means Luke is espousing "sloppy theology"; it simply means that biblically our relationship with the Holy Spirit can be variously described. From this then we see that to be "filled with the Spirit" or "to have the Holy Spirit poured out in our lives" or "to be baptized with the Holy Spirit" (beyond initial placement into Christ's body as discussed in Lesson 1) basically describe the selfsame event, namely, "to receive from Jesus' hand divine power—the same power He Himself experienced—for living and serving and to have the Holy Spirit poured into us."[3]

In Acts 6:1–6 we meet seven extraordinary men given a special assignment. What was their special assignment? What do the apostles state as a necessary prerequisite to fulfilling this assignment? (v. 3)

What does Acts 11:24 say was a specific factor in Barnabas's successful exhortation to the church in Antioch?

Read Acts 13:48–52. What is recorded here as happening to Paul and Barnabas at the hands of some of the Jews? How did they respond? What is given as a specific factor in their ability to so respond? (v. 52)

THE BAPTISM IN THE HOLY SPIRIT

It is generally conceded that Luke is not only a valid historian, but that his reporting of history gives us valid theology. In other words, as we look at Acts we see *how* believers initially encounter the Spirit *and* His fullness; from Luke's theology of how to initially encounter the Spirit's fullness, Paul then instructs us in the ongoing daily walk (Rom. 8:1–8; Eph. 5:18). Some term Luke's theology of encountering the Spirit's *fullness* as "the baptism in the Holy Spirit" whose primary purpose is for additional power to service humanity.

However we may phrase the Lucan accounts, what can we note from the following passages in Acts about the Spirit's anointing believers for power, especially to witness? (1:8) Any common threads?

2:4

10:44–46

19:6

SPIRIT-FILLED FOR A PURPOSE

As noted above, one of the purposes of the fullness of the Holy Spirit in our lives is to better service humanity. Hence, Jesus' clear statement that "when the Holy Spirit has come upon you . . . you shall be witnesses to Me" (Acts 1:8). Read the following passages in Acts and note the specific activity associated with the fullness of the Holy Spirit.

Acts 6:5, 8

Acts 8:6, 7

Acts 8:26–29

Acts 8:39, 40

Acts 13:2

Acts 16:6–8

BEHIND THE SCENES

Mark 16:14–18 is what is sometimes called "a disputed text. "That is, there are differing opinions among biblical textual scholars as to whether it was part of Mark's original manuscript or was added later by a copyist. There is, however, significant evidence to support it as inspired Scripture. Examine, for example, the words of R. C. Lenski, the great Lutheran scholar:

As to the internal evidence, the question is this: "Do these last verses betray the fact that Mark did not write them, or are their language and their character such as show that Mark could not have written them?" We unhesitatingly answer in the negative. Already the general admission of the critics is significant that the conclusion of the Gospel shows careful consideration and harmonizes well with its beginning, especially in this that the apostles are ordered to go and preach the gospel in all the world, and that they indeed did this. But this is rather strong evidence for Mark's composition of this so fitting conclusion. The better the conclusion fits, the more likely it is that it stems from Mark; the reverse cannot be held.[4]

What do these words of Jesus therefore promise that further supports Luke's reportings?

 WORD WEALTH

Baptism, *baptisma.* The essential meaning of "baptism" is to be immersed into something; a person "baptized" in water becomes fully immersed in the water. The baptism in the Holy Spirit, then, is being fully immersed into the life of Jesus Christ, allowing Him to have maximum control in our lives. That control then manifests itself in our moral life-style, our devotion to God and our service for Him. Bringing together what we've learned so far in our two lessons, it is obvious that the New Testament writers, especially Luke, want us to see the parallel between the work of the Spirit in Jesus' life and the life of His disciples.

 BEHIND THE SCENES

Two passages in Acts are subject to great diversity of interpretation in evangelical Christendom relative to the baptism in the Holy Spirit. They are Acts 8:14–17 and 19:1–7. Using two or three scholarly commentaries that address the controversies, learn the points of conflict and how evangelicalism handles the diversity. Of particular value are John Stott's *The Spirit, the Church, and the World* (Downers Grove, IL: InterVarsity Press, 1990) and Roger Stronstad's *The Charismatic Theology of St. Luke* (Peabody, MA: Hendrickson Publishers, 1984).

SO HOW DO WE ENCOUNTER HIS FULLNESS?

Our natural tendency to want to "work" for God's free gifts makes it necessary to look at how we encounter and maintain the Spirit in His fullness. The words of Paul to the Galatians must stay before us: "This only I want to learn from you: Did you receive the Spirit by the works of the law, or by the hearing of faith? Are you so foolish? Having begun in the Spirit, are you now being made perfect by the flesh? Have you suffered so many things in vain—if indeed *it was* in vain? Therefore He who supplies the Spirit to you and works miracles among you, *does* He do *it* by the works of the law, or by the hearing of faith?" (3:2–5)

Let's see how this principle is modeled in Acts.

To what does Peter attribute the initial filling with the Holy Spirit? (11:17)

How did the Samaritans receive the Holy Spirit and His fullness? (8:12, 17)

What was Peter talking about when "the Holy Spirit fell upon all those who heard the word"? (10:43, 44)

This does not mean we are totally passive; the fullness of the Holy Spirit in the lives of New Testament persons is clearly tied into a couple of other important elements. Read the following passages and note what one such element is.

Luke 3:21, 22

Luke 11:13

Acts 4:23–31

Acts 8:15

Read the following passages and note another important element.

John 14:15–17

Acts 5:32

BRINGING TOGETHER PAUL AND LUKE

As stated above, Luke shows us how to initially encounter the Spirit's fullness; and Paul instructs us in the ongoing daily walk, which includes "continuously being filled with the Holy Spirit" (Eph. 5:18) and learning to live in Him. Let's explore Romans 8:1–8 to see what we can discover about daily life in the Spirit.

Life in the Spirit sets us free from what? (v. 2)

What is the only way this becomes possible? (v. 3)

What is to be the daily focal point of those *"who live according to the Spirit"*? (v. 5)

What is a fruit of living in the Spirit? (v. 6)

 FAITH ALIVE

How would you summarize your findings in this chapter? Does it not seem to you that God wants us to move beyond initial Spirit baptism into Christ Jesus into a fuller, ongoing relationship in the Holy Spirit? What do the passages in Acts seem to indicate about the quality of this dynamic life in the Spirit? about some expected manifestations? What do you see in Romans about the ongoing life of the Spirit that you'd like to see more fully developed in your life? What further power demonstrations of His fullness would you like to see in your life?

1. *Spirit-Filled Life Bible* (Nashville, TN: Thomas Nelson Publishers, 1991), 1588, note on 7:38.
2. Ibid., 1794, note on 5:18.
3. Jack Hayford, *Spirit-Filled* (Wheaton, IL: Tyndale House Publishers, Inc., 1987), 7.
4. R. C. Lenski, *The Interpretation of St. Mark's Gospel* (St. Louis, MO: Concordia Publishing House, 1946, 1961), 755.

Lesson 3/ *The Greatest of These Is Love*

Have you ever known someone to be used mightily of God and yet you sensed a need for some additional love or character refinement in his/her life? This is Paul's concern in 1 Corinthians 13. He knows that it is possible to have the manifestations of the Spirit operate without the fruit of love, stating quite clearly that he can "speak with the tongues of men and of angels, but have not love," or he can "have *the gift of* prophecy . . . but have not love" (vv. 1, 2). Yet, though such be possible, it undermines God's intent. The manifestation of tongues without the fruit of love makes one "become sounding brass or a clanging cymbal" (v. 1); prophecy without love makes one "nothing " (v. 2).

Love-motivated manifestations of the Spirit is what Paul means by saying he'll show us "a more excellent way" (1 Cor. 12:31). "'A more excellent way' is not a negative comparison between gifts and love, since the temporal adverb 'yet' indicates the continuation of the subject. All manifestations of the Spirit must at the same time manifest the ways of love, for love is the ultimate issue behind all things."[1] The Corinthians were obviously dynamic in spiritual manifestations, but weak in the very fruit that enables the gifts to ultimately be "for the profit of all" (12:7).

Paul then is not pitting the fruit against the gifts. Such a thought would cause him to shudder. It's GIFTS and LOVE, LOVE and GIFTS. It's a matter of learning to minister with a proper attitude, a tremendous harmony in which the beauty of character is interwoven with the power of dynamic ministry. There is probably nothing more destructive to the power of the Holy Spirit in our lives than self-interest. When we divorce the ethics of the fruit, especially love, from the ministry of the

Spirit, we're on a collision course—no matter how "anointed" we might appear. "Since the basis of all gifts is love, that spirit of love is the qualifying factor for biblical exercise of the gifts of the Holy Spirit. Thus, those in authority must 'try the spirits' to assure that those who exercise spiritual gifts actually 'follow after love' as well as 'desire spiritual gifts.'"[2] Let's see what we can learn then from an exploration of 1 Corinthians 12—14.

LET'S NOT BE IGNORANT!

Each of us likely has assumptions regarding the use of the gifts of the Spirit. Rarely do we come to Christ without some theological or practical focal point. Unfortunately, our experiential or preferred practice often forms our doctrinal understanding of how to operate in the manifestations of the Spirit. This was the problem at Corinth. They had their pagan rituals as models for "spiritual manifestations"; they formed the basis of their model for "a truly 'spiritual' meeting." Their hearts were right and their manifestations were of the Spirit, but their motive and method were similar to those of frenzied heathen! Paul's first concern is to contrast their former experiences as pagans with Christian truth. Let's see how Paul refocuses them—and us.

What is a necessary prerequisite if we want to be used in the gifts of the Spirit? (1 Cor. 12:1)

What must we realize could be the case with our presuppositions and/or previous spiritual experiences regarding the use of spiritual gifts? (1 Cor. 12:2, 3)

Paul then is setting the stage for ministering in the powerful manifestations of the Spirit. We must be well taught biblically, and we must thoroughly examine our preconceived notions of how to move in the Spirit.

BEHIND THE SCENES

The pagan background of the Corinthians gave them one definition of being "spiritual"; Paul had another. Their focal point was their pagan rituals in which they were "carried away to these dumb idols" (12:2); Paul's focal point is the truth that "Jesus is Lord" (12:3) and that all manifestations of the Holy Spirit are subject to self-control (14:28–32).

Pagan worship was very frenzied. The Greek words translated "carried away" (12:2) are intensive, suggesting times in ecstatic heathen worship when a person is believed to be possessed by a supernatural force. The New Testament would see this as demonic ravishing (cf. 1 Cor. 10:20). Realizing that demonic or fleshly forces can in part imitate true manifestations of the Spirit, Paul calls in 1 Corinthians 12—14 for analyzation of their Christian enthusiasm in worship.

Power and gifts are not the ultimate tribute to the Spirit's presence. According to 1 Corinthians 12:3, what is?

What must be the chief purpose for desiring to be used in the gifts of the Spirit? (1 Cor. 12:7)

Realizing the vulnerability of the human ego in seeking after the Spirit's manifestations, what is Paul's point in 1 Corinthians 12:11?

In 1 Corinthians 13:4 we read, "Love does not envy." How does 1 Corinthians 12:12–26 illustrate this idea?

SIXTEEN NOBLE ASPECTS

Although love will be studied in detail in our next lesson, certain aspects of Paul's sixteenfold definition of love in 1 Corinthians 13:4–8a highlight our current emphasis—ministering in Holy Spirit fullness "for the profit *of all*" (12:7). He does so by telling us what love is *not*. Let's see what God's Word notes in 1 Corinthians 13:4, 5.

1. "Love does not parade itself" (v. 4). The idea here is that of not behaving as a windbag, of not falsely bragging. According to 1 Corinthians 8:1, 2, what's one way we're tempted to falsely brag?

What does James 4:13–17 say is another temptation point?

2. "Love . . . is not puffed up" (1 Cor. 13:4). False pride was a problem in Corinth. Read these verses in 1 Corinthians and note how they were falsely puffing themselves up.

4:6

4:18, 19

5:1, 2

8:1, 2

3. "Love . . . does not behave rudely" (13:4, 5). The idea here is that of behaving shamefully. It is translated in 7:36 as "behaving improperly" (NKJV). What is its context there? How does its use there further illuminate Paul's intent here?

4. "Love . . . does not seek its own" (13:4, 5). We are not to be enamored with self-gain or self-worth. In 1 Corinthians 10:23–33 Paul proposes one way to battle self-focus. What is it?

What is one way Christ modeled this principle of not seeking His own? (Rom. 15:1–3)

 FAITH ALIVE

Love, then, is behaving exactly opposite of our natural, egocentric Adamic nature. Can you see the obvious correlation then between the need to wed love and the gifts? Can you identify any potential points of "ego vulnerability" in your own life when it comes to manifestations of the Spirit? If so, write them down and pray about them until you sense God is truly bringing change.

 KINGDOM EXTRA

In Acts 8:9–24, Luke examples a person seeking the Spirit's power for the wrong reasons. Study that section carefully, noting the reason for Simon's request and Peter's assessment of his root problem.

LOVE IN ACTION

Jesus came to demonstrate God's love to mankind, to show us how to love "for the profit *of all*" (1 Cor. 12:7). Read the following scriptures and note how in part He demonstrates this "others-focused love."

Mark 10:21

John 11:5–16

John 13:1

Gal. 2:20

Phil. 2:5–11

Most scholars agree that this Philippians passage is part of an ancient Christian hymn. As such, it demonstrates the long-standing heritage of exalting the giving, servanthood nature of Jesus. He was "equal with God" but chose not to cling to that position for personal advantage—a true testimony that He was indeed "filled with the Holy Spirit" (Luke 4:1).

What does the Bible say about us showing this same love to others?

Matt. 22:39

1 Pet. 1:22

1 John 3:16

1 John 3:18

FAITH ALIVE

Before proceeding, stop and ponder Jesus' model and the New Testament's call for demonstrated love to others. Remember, our chief purpose in this lesson is to develop a proper servant's attitude for Spirit-empowered ministry. It's an integral part of fulfilling Paul's command to "earnestly desire the best gifts" (1 Cor. 12:31). Can you list two or three people whom God would have you more effectively serve in love? "Let each of you look out not only for his own interests, but also for the interests of others" (Phil. 2:4).

WORD WEALTH

Desire, *zeloo.* To be zealous for, to burn with desire, to pursue ardently, to desire eagerly or intensely. Negatively, the word is associated with strong envy and jealousy (Acts 7:9; 17:5; 1 Cor. 13:4; James 4:2).[3]

KINGDOM EXTRA

If you have a Bible dictionary or encyclopedia, read the article on "spiritual gifts." Then, as you have time, carefully reread 1 Corinthians 12:12–26, along with Romans 12:3–8 and 1 Peter 4:10, 11. Do you see any common attitudes addressed? What undeniable conclusion can we draw regarding the need for mutual interdependence in the operation of spiritual gifts in the church?

ARE WE GETTING THE POINT?

When 1 Corinthians was originally written, there were no chapter designations. Therefore, chapters 12—14 formed a single unit with a unified purpose. Let's trace Paul's underlying thread and see how his contrast of "tongues" and "prophecy" illustrates his bigger point that love-empowered manifestations of the Spirit must always serve to minister to the needs of others. Let's do our best to get the point!

What does 1 Corinthians 14:1 clarify about God's view of the gifts and the fruit of the Holy Spirit?

Read 1 Corinthians 13 carefully. In context, what do you suppose is Paul's point in verse 8b?

First Corinthians 13:11 is Paul's way of illustrating the principle of verses 9 and 10. What is the point of his illustration?

The present and future economies of God are radically different with respect to the gifts. It's just like the change of behavior between childhood and adulthood. Gifts are instruments for ministry and gospel advancement, and, as such, are vitally appropriate and important to church life now; but they are only for now. In the "Eschaton"—the ultimate end, that is, "the last thing"—it's our character that will shine forth and endure, so we should never opt for gifts without love. It is this enduring aspect of love that makes it "the greatest" (1 Cor. 13:13).

WORD WEALTH

Endures, *hupomeno.* To hold one's ground in conflict, bear up against adversity, hold out under stress, stand firm, persevere under pressure, wait calmly and courageously. It is not passive resignation to fate and mere patience, but the active, energetic resistance to defeat that allows calm and brave endurance.[4]

AT A GLANCE

A More Excellent Way (1 Cor. 13:1–13)[5]		
Love is . . .	Without Love . . .	Love is Greater Than . . .
Patient, kind, unselfish, truthful, hopeful, enduring (vv. 4–7) Not envious, proud, self-centered, rude, or provoked to anger (vv. 4, 5)	Tongues are mere noise (v.1) Prophecy, mysteries, knowledge, and faith amount to nothing (v. 2) Good deeds are unprofitable (v. 3)	Prophecies, which will fail (v. 8) Tongues, which will cease (v. 8) Knowledge, which will vanish (v. 8)
Love is one of the dynamic terms Paul uses to speak of the holy life enabled by the fullness of the Holy Spirit. It encompasses motive and deed. Love is characteristic of the mature believer.		

PROPHECY AND TONGUES

Paul chooses to contrast tongues and prophecy in 1 Corinthians 14 to illustrate this matter of watching our attitude and intent for wanting to demonstrate spiritual manifestations.

In this light, what does Paul mean in 14:20 by when he writes, "Do not be children in understanding"?

According to 14:3, why does one prophesy?

According to 14:4, why does one speak in tongues?

Is this a worthy or desirable purpose for speaking in tongues? (See Jude 20.)

Is Paul saying in 14:2–5, then, that prophecy *per se* is greater than tongues? What light does verse 19 shed on this topic?

"Paul's endorsement of prophecy over tongues in corporate gatherings is qualified by his equating the *value* of tongues with prophecy, if the tongue is accompanied by interpretation. Therefore, tongues without interpretation are for personal edification. Prophecy and tongues with interpretation minister to the entire congregation, being understood by all."[6]

 PROBING THE DEPTHS

A key point of controversy in the church is understanding when it is that "prophecies . . . will fail . . . tongues . . . will cease . . . knowledge . . . will vanish away" (1 Cor. 13:8). "Will fail" and "will vanish away" translate the same Greek verb *(katargeo)*; "will cease" translates an interchangeable verb *(pauomai)* used for rhetorical purposes. In 2:6 Paul uses *katargeo* to describe "the rulers of this age, who are <u>coming to</u>

nothing"; in 6:13 *katargeo* describes the destruction God will bring to both food and the stomach; in 15:24–26 it describes the time when "He puts an end to all rule and all authority and power."

Did any of these things happen with the death of the apostles or canonizing of the Bible? Obviously not. Does it not seem then that Paul would be consistent and that the cessation of which he speaks in 13:8 is the end of this age, the consummation of the Kingdom? In other words, tongues (indeed, all the gifts as such) *will* pass away, but not until their purpose and manifest need for ministry has been fulfilled. This will not be until Christ comes again for His church.

 FAITH ALIVE

Ready to take an "inventory check"? In Lesson 2 we sought a fuller baptism into the Holy Spirit's life, especially His manifestations. Are we now ready to pray for an increased attitude of love with which to minister? How would you grade your "love" barometer?

1. *Spirit-Filled Life Bible* (Nashville, TN: Thomas Nelson Publishers, 1991), 1739, note on 12:31.

2. Ibid., 1739, "Kingdom Dynamics: Love: The Qualifying Factor."

3. Ibid., 1740, "Word Wealth: 14:1 desire."

4. Ibid., 1451, "Word Wealth: 24:13 endures."

5. *The Wesley Bible* (Nashville, TN: Thomas Nelson Publishers, 1990), 1732, "Chart: A More Excellent Way (1 Cor. 13:1–13)."

6. *Spirit-Filled Life Bible*, 1741, note on 14:5.

Lesson 4/Love, Joy, and Peace

Remember the last time you visited an exquisite, well-stocked and well-maintained fruit stand? Chances are you found the fruit inviting—maybe even compelling! (Ever been tempted to snitch a grape or two?) There's just something wonderfully inviting about good fruit.

Our next three lessons will focus on the nine major characteristics of the fruit of the Spirit listed in Galatians 5:22, 23. Each of the nine aspects has a relational dynamic to it; in other words, the fruit describes how each of us can better "look out not only for his own interests, but also for the interests of others" (Phil. 2:4). Its cultivation in our lives counters "the works of the flesh . . . uncleanness, lewdness . . . hatred . . . jealousies . . . selfish ambitions" (Gal. 5:19, 20).

The fruit then represents the sanctifying work of the Spirit in our lives. It's part of our ongoing walk with Him; it is not a special gift or manifestation. The very terminology "fruit" depicts this; fruit grows as the result of life. "And this I pray, that your love may abound still more and more in knowledge and all discernment . . . being filled with the fruits of righteousness which *are* by Jesus Christ" (Phil. 1:9, 11). The manifestations of the Spirit are indeed powerful; but so is the fruit—witness to a transformed life.

"Being filled with the Spirit calls us as much to character as it does to charismatic activity. The Holy Spirit's fruit is to be grown in our lives every bit as much as His gifts may be shown through us."[1] Let's discover what His ninefold fruit is all about and how it's developed in our lives; we'll then examine the nine major manifestations of the Spirit.

FIRST, HOW DO WE GET THIS FRUIT?

Before looking specifically at each of the aspects of the fruit, it's important that we grasp how it's developed in our lives. With regard to this, Paul makes an interesting comment in Galatians 5:23 when he says, "Against such there is no law." By this he likely means that the fruit cannot be legally demanded nor produced. A tree does not bear fruit by an act of Congress! It is the result of our divine life in Christ. Let's see what the New Testament says about this matter.

Carefully read John 15:1–11 and answer the following:

What is a necessary prerequisite in our lives before the fruit can even begin to be developed? (v. 3)

What act of ours is absolutely essential to its development? (vv. 4, 5)

What crucial element is part of the Father's process for cultivating the fruit in our lives? (v. 2)

What is the Father's will regarding the fruit in our lives? (v. 8)

The fruit of the Spirit then develops only as we stay in close association with Jesus Christ. Encouraged by the fact Jesus is remaining in union with us (v. 4), we're called to remain in close union with Him. This alone enables us to bear "much fruit; for without Me you can do nothing" (v. 5).

In Colossians 3:10 we're told to "put on the new *man*." What are we then told about this new man that further explains the development of God's fruit in our lives?

KINGDOM EXTRA

What does it mean biblically to "abide"? Is it an active or passive word? Does the "abiding" manifest itself in any practical ways? The primary Greek word translated "abide" (*meno*) has the idea of staying in place with someone, remaining steadfast or especially near to someone. The model is that of Jesus Christ and the Holy Spirit who, "descending from heaven like a dove . . . remained [*meno*] upon Him" (John 1:32). Ponder the following scriptures and write down what you observe from each by way of a fuller understanding of "abiding in Christ."

John 6:56

1 John 2:6–11

1 John 2:17

WHAT THE WORLD NEEDS NOW IS LOVE

Though the above phrase was popularized and somewhat trivialized by a "pop" song in the late sixties, it is nonetheless true. The world does need love—God's love. Paul begins his nine-point listing with "love"—*agape* in Greek—God's special attitude leading to benevolent action; the very quality He wants perfected in His children; a major pillar upon which the Christian life is built. The obvious importance of "love" in the Bible is seen in the fact that "God is love" (1 John 4:8), that He "so loved the world that He gave His only begotten Son" (John 3:16) and that "the greatest of these *is* love" (1 Cor. 13:13).

Read the following to see what more we can learn about love.

Luke 6:27

Col. 3:14

1 Pet. 4:8

1 John 3:18

✎ WORD WEALTH

Love, *agape.* A word to which Christianity gave new meaning. Outside of the New Testament, it rarely occurs in existing Greek manuscripts of the period. *Agape* denotes an undefeatable benevolence and unconquerable goodwill that always seeks the highest good of the other person, no matter what he does. It is the self-giving love that gives freely without asking anything in return, and does not consider the worth of its object. *Agape* . . . refers to the will rather than the emotion. *Agape* describes the unconditional love God has for the world.[2] There are two other major words in *koine* Greek for "love"—*eros* and *philos. Eros* is used basically for passionate love which desires another for oneself and seeks to transport one beyond rationality, often through intoxication. We get our English "erotic" from it. *Philos* is an inclination toward or solicitous love of gods for men or friends for friends, although in the New Testament the distinction between *agape* and *philos* sometimes blurs. For example, John sometimes uses *philos* and *agape* interchangeably to describe God's love for Jesus (John 3:35; 5:20) and for His children (John 3:16; 16:27).

AT A GLANCE

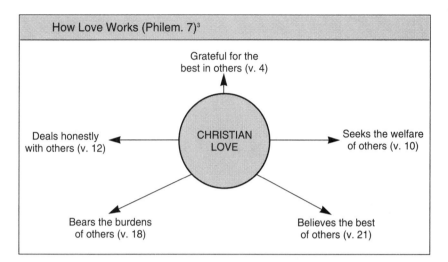

How Love Works (Philem. 7)[3]

Grateful for the
best in others (v. 4)

Deals honestly
with others (v. 12)

CHRISTIAN
LOVE

Seeks the welfare
of others (v. 10)

Bears the burdens
of others (v. 18)

Believes the best
of others (v. 21)

BACK TO 1 CORINTHIANS 13

In our last lesson we examined four of the sixteen characteristics of love listed in 1 Corinthians 13:4–8a. Let's go back and pick up the others.

1. "Love suffers long *and* is kind" (v. 4)—to be covered in our next lesson under the fourth and fifth aspects of the fruit—longsuffering and kindness.

2. "Love does not envy" (v. 4)—The idea here is that of not being motivated by rivalry or competition. According to Acts 17:1–9, what can happen if envy prevails?

3. "Love . . . is not provoked" (vv. 4, 5)—The idea is that of not being easily provoked to anger by others. According to Acts 15:36–41, Paul and Barnabas on one occasion did provoke each other. What was the result?

4. "Love . . . thinks no evil" (vv. 4, 5)—The idea is that of not keeping a record of wrong done to someone by someone else. How did Jesus model this in Luke 23:34?

5. "Love . . . does not rejoice in iniquity, but rejoices in the truth" (vv. 4, 6)—The idea is that of morally aligning oneself with the truth of the gospel, of refusing to be delighted by any kind of evil (cf. Rom. 12:9). According to Romans 12:14–21, what are some ways in which we can practice this truth?

6. "Love . . . bears all things . . . endures all things" (vv. 4, 7)—The idea is that love can face anything at any time. Read 1 Corinthians 4:8–13 and note how this functioned in Paul's life.

7. "Love . . . believes all things, hopes all things" (vv. 4, 7)—The idea is that love never stops believing in the mercy of God at work in life and its circumstances. This same truth was taught at length to the Romans in Romans 8:31–39. What can we learn there about believing in God's mercy working in our lives?

8. "Love never fails" (v. 8a)—See under "Are We Getting the Point?" in Lesson 3.

SOMEHOW I'VE LOST MY JOY!
Has Anybody Found It?

So much of the joy we experience in this life seems to be transitory—lasting only for a short time. And yet Jesus says, "These things I have spoken to you, that My joy may remain in you, and *that* your joy may be full" (John 15:11). Let's see what lasting joy is all about.

 **WORD WEALTH**

Joy, *chara.* In the New Testament *chara* is found only in a relationship with Jesus Christ (Rom. 5:11). It is the assurance that we are members of God's family regardless of what positives or negatives life brings (Luke 10:17–20; Rom. 8:38, 39). It is closely aligned with *hope,* which is the confident assurance that God is ultimately in control and will someday right all wrongs with the return of Jesus Christ (Titus 2:13).

What other virtues does Paul associate with joy in Colossians 1:11?

What role did joy play in Jesus' crucifixion? (Heb. 12:2)

What strengthens joy? (James 1:2)

What is the one thing that brings about "joy inexpressible"? (1 Pet. 1:8)

What is one way this sure foundation of joy can express itself? (2 Cor. 8:2)

Joy, then, is that ever-deepening awareness that our lives are hidden in Christ and that we can be led by the Spirit through anything. Afflictions, trials, pressures or frustrations may come, but they cannot destroy us; so we experience joy. We may genuinely hurt (2 Cor. 1:8), we may weep (John 11:33–35), we may be tempted (Heb. 2:18), we may not understand what God is allowing to come our way (James 1:2–5); but none of this causes us to lose God's focus in our life. We can even look beyond our own circumstances during difficulties and minister to the needs of others. "We know that all things work together for good to those who love God, to those who are the called according to *His* purpose" (Rom. 8:28). This is biblical joy.

LONGING FOR PEACE

The human heart longs for peace; Jesus promises it (John 14:27), and the Spirit longs to develop it. Our positional "peace with God" (Rom. 5:1) ushers in the possibility of "the peace of God . . . [guarding our] hearts and minds through Christ Jesus" (Phil. 4:7). Let's see what this entails.

 WORD WEALTH

Peace, *eirene.* Compare "irenic" and "Irene." A state of rest, quietness, and calmness; an absence of strife; tranquility. It generally denotes a perfect well-being. *Eirene* includes harmonious relationships between God and men, men and men, nations, and families. Jesus as Prince of Peace gives peace to those who call upon Him for personal salvation.[4]

What is God's provision for peace in our lives? (Col. 1:20)

What must we truly love to experience great peace? (Ps. 119:165)

Read the following scriptures and note where God wants peace to be found:

Rom. 12:18

1 Cor. 7:15

1 Cor. 14:33

What is Paul's command concerning peace in Romans 14:19?

What does Jesus promise those who strive for peace? (Matt. 5:9)

Peace then has to do with personal wholeness and beneficial relationships. It is an inward assurance that because we are positionally righteous with God by grace through faith in Jesus

Christ, we have access to His powers to touch all facets of our lives. Hence Hebrews 13:20, 21 says, "Now may the God of peace . . . make you complete in every good work to do His will," so that life's relationships and circumstances reflect God's intent rather than that of selfish flesh.

BEHIND THE SCENES

Eirene in the New Testament has its roots in the Old Testament *shalom* which has as its root meaning the idea "well-being" in all areas of life—health, wealth, success, and security.[5] Although the degree to which some of the particulars of *shalom* comprise part of a New Testament life of *eirene* is subject to much debate, one thing is clear linguistically—the New Testament writers inherited a basic Jewish meaning of *eirene;* we do well to remember this as we study the New Testament.

FAITH ALIVE

What has all this said to you personally? Can you define clearly how the fruit of the Spirit is developed? Can you target a couple of people in prayer to love (to show undefeatable benevolence and unconquerable goodwill) more effectively? Can you identify anything that's robbing you of your joy (the assurance your life is hidden in Christ and that you can be led by the Spirit through anything)? What do you suppose you need to do about it? Would you say your life is characterized mostly by peace (personal wholeness and beneficial relationships) or chaos? Seriously consider these matters and take them to prayer regularly with a special concentration for at least the next month.

1. *Spirit-Filled Life Bible* (Nashville, TN: Thomas Nelson Publishers, 1991), 1780, "Kingdom Dynamics: A Call to Character."

2. Ibid., 1694, "Word Wealth: 5:5 love."

3. *The Wesley Bible* (Nashville, TN: Thomas Nelson Publishers, 1990), 1840, "Chart: How Love Works (Philem. 7)."

4. *Spirit-Filled Life Bible,* 1510, "Word Wealth: 1:79 peace."

5. C. F. Evans, in *A Theological Word Book of the Bible,* ed. Alan Richardson (New York, NY: Macmillan Publishing Co., Inc., 1977), 165.

Lesson 5/ Longsuffering, Kindness, and Goodness

Ever feel like you've exhausted your ability to be understanding? Ever feel like you just don't have any more "grace" to extend to someone? Ever struggled with being generous with others? Ever wish others would extend more understanding, grace, and generosity to you?

If the truth of these realities intrigues you, our current lesson is custom-made! As we delve into the next triad of the fruit of the Spirit—longsuffering, kindness, and goodness—we'll see that it's a study in understanding, as well as [otherwise, not parallel] gracious and generous living. It's a call from the Spirit to learn to interface with others in the same manner God interfaces with us!

"You know, Pastor," says the young husband struggling in his new marital relationship, "if I were truly honest with myself, I'd have to admit I don't want to treat her as graciously as God treats me. Quite frankly, I'm so hurt and we've struggled so much in our relationship, I sort of want 'grace for myself' and 'judgment for her'! I know it's wrong, but that's how I feel."

"You know, Pastor," says the corporate executive, "it seems my generosity is going unnoticed these days; I think I'm going to fire the whole lot of them and let them try to find another CEO as generous as I. I know we're not supposed to give with strings attached or give to get back, but I'm quite frankly ready to take matters into my own hands. Even if I don't end up firing them, let's see if they get a bonus this Christmas."

"Not even a turkey?"

"Not even a turkey . . . pretty bad attitude, huh?"

Both of these men are right in that they know they're wrong; nonetheless, such attitudes are real in the lives of many Christians. It's part of the battle waged between the Spirit and the flesh, which "are contrary to one another, so that [we] do not do the things that [we] wish" (Gal. 5:17). It's a manifestation of the judgmental selfishness of the works of the flesh which the fruit of the Spirit is out to counter. So this triad of the fruit of the Spirit gets down to basics—learning to deal with others exactly as our understanding, gracious, and generous heavenly Father deals with us. In each of these characteristics of the fruit of the Spirit, He becomes the Model that His Spirit longs to develop in us.

Ready to crucify a bit more of "the flesh with its passions and desires" (Gal. 5:24)? Then let's proceed and see what God's word has to say about the next three aspects of the fruit of the Spirit.

LONG-TEMPERED OR SHORT-FUSED?

 WORD WEALTH

Patience, *makrothumia.* From *makros,* "long," and *thumos,* "temper." The word denotes lenience, forbearance, fortitude, patient endurance, longsuffering. Also included in *makrothumia* is the ability to endure persecution and ill-treatment. It describes a person who has the power to exercise revenge but instead exercises restraint.[1] It characterizes true, godly love, for "love suffers long" (1 Cor. 13:4).

What do each of the following scriptures teach about God's or Jesus' longsuffering?

Rom. 9:19–26, especially v. 22

1 Tim. 1:15, 16

2 Pet. 3:9

God's longsuffering knows how to balance justice and mercy. It is always redemptive in nature, with the goal of bringing people to repentance (Rom. 2:4).[2]

FIRST GOD, NOW US

What does 2 Timothy 4:2 say about longsuffering in the life of church leaders?

According to 2 Corinthians 6:3–10 and 2 Timothy 3:10, 11, in what life circumstance are we likely to find an understanding of what it means to be longsuffering?

Do you have a special promise from God for which you're waiting? What does Hebrews 6:12, 15 teach about the process often involved in inheriting such promises?

 KINGDOM EXTRA

A key to understanding the New Testament concept of longsuffering is the Old Testament's understanding of God's *hesed,* Hebrew for "steadfast love, mercy or demonstrations of faithfulness based on covenant agreement." Study the following scriptures to glean what you can about covenant and God's *hesed*.

1 Kin. 8:22–24

Ps. 89:28, 49

Is. 55:3

How are God's longsuffering and *hesed* demonstrated in Hosea?

A valuable extra resource is also the article on "Mercy" in *Synonyms of the Old Testament: Numerically Coded to Strong's Exhaustive Concordance,* by Robert Girdlestone (Grand Rapids, MI: Baker Book House, 1983).

PUT ON LONGSUFFERING

Paul often urges us to live out our relationship with God in terms of longsuffering toward others. Read the following scriptures and note his specific imperatives.

Eph. 4:1–3

Col. 3:12

1 Thess. 5:12–15

What further light does Colossians 1:11 shed on Paul's understanding of the development of longsuffering in our lives?

 FAITH ALIVE

We can conclude then that the longsuffering the Spirit wants to develop in us is the same longsuffering repeatedly seen in God. The way in which God extended and still extends Himself to us in Christ is how we are to extend our-selves to each other in Him. It's inseparable from love (Eph. 4:2), and it knows how to balance "justice and mercy." In short, it's a work of the Spirit whereby we long to gain insight into another's actions and respond with that insight in mind rather than responding hastily in judgment.

Would you agree right now with God to have Him further develop longsuffering in your character? How about even making a list of some specific people toward whom you could demonstrate more longsuffering? It's vital to effective, Spirit-filled living.

"REMEMBER, BE GRACIOUS"

Remember those words from dear old Mom or some other person responsible for training you in proper attitudes and social skills? They meant, "Be kind and favorable, even though you probably don't want to!" This is what biblical *kindness* is all about—acting with godly graciousness toward others, even if we're inclined to do otherwise.

 WORD WEALTH

Kindness, *chrestotes.* Goodness in action, sweetness of disposition, gentleness in dealing with others, benevolence, kindness, affability. The word describes the ability to act for the welfare of those taxing your patience. The Holy Spirit removes abrasive qualities from the character of one under His control.[3]

According to Romans 11:22, who receives God's kindness?

According to Ephesians 2:7, what is one way in which God will show "the exceeding riches of His grace" toward believers "in the ages to come"?

According to Titus 3:4, 5, what is one way God's kindness is manifest?

What can we learn from Romans 3:12 about kindness and unredeemed humankind?

According to Colossians 3:12, 13, what application are the redeemed to make of the kindness developed in them by the Spirit?

According to Ephesians 4:31, 32, what are some ways we can demonstrate kindness or graciousness toward others?

What does Luke 6:35 teach us about the kindness of God that serves as a model to our interfacing with ungracious or selfish people who might appear to be our enemies?

SACRIFICIAL GENEROSITY

Remember the old proverb, "It is easy to be generous with other people's money"? That well depicts the attitude of natural man—it's okay to be generous, so long as it doesn't require much self-sacrifice! Not so with our next fruit of the Spirit—*goodness,* the fruit of dealing generously with others.

 WORD WEALTH

Goodness, *agathosune.* Compare "Agatha" and possibly "agate." Beneficence, kindness in actual manifestation, virtue equipped for action, a bountiful propensity both to will and to do what is good, intrinsic goodness producing a generosity and a Godlike state or being. *Agathosune* is a rare word that combines being good and doing good.[4]

Who alone is our Source of goodness? (Matt. 19:16, 17)

What do 1 Chronicles 16:34 and 2 Chronicles 5:13 further teach us about the nature of God?

According to Nahum 1:7, why is "the LORD . . . a stronghold in the day of trouble"?

The goodness of God always leads to action in human history as evidenced by the fact that He gave Israel "many good *things*" (Neh. 9:35) and by the fact that "every good gift and every perfect gift is from above, and comes down from the Father of lights" (James 1:17).

PROBING THE DEPTHS

Psalm 107:1 says, "Oh, give thanks to the LORD, for *He is* good." It then goes on to list several reasons why He is good. Carefully read the entire psalm and note several demonstrations of His goodness.

Having established that the goodness of God leads to His doing good works, let's now look at His goodness producing good works in us.

According to Romans 7:19, however, what do we need to remember whenever we want to do acts of goodness?

According to Ephesians 2:10, why should we expect ourselves to do many acts of goodness?

According to Romans 15:14, how did the Romans in part bring satisfaction to Paul?

According to Matthew 12:35, from whence do good works come?

According to Matthew 5:16, what results from our doing good works?

 KINGDOM EXTRA

Biblically, the opposite of *goodness* is *envy*. With the help of a Bible dictionary or New Testament Greek word study book, study the concept of *envy*. (Note especially Matt. 27:18; Phil. 1:15; Titus 3:3.) What can you learn from this opposite vice about the virtue of *goodness?*

 FAITH ALIVE

See any possible area for spiritual growth? Can you target some specific people toward whom you'd like to grow in demonstrating longsuffering (lenience through understanding), kindness (gentleness in dealing with others) or goodness (doing acts of generosity)? If so, then agree with yourself and possibly two or three others to make this a matter of prayer and concentration in the days ahead. Perhaps you could pray Paul's prayer for the Thessalonians for each other, "We also pray always for you that our God would count you worthy of *this* calling, and fulfill all the good pleasure of *His* goodness and the work of faith with power" (2 Thess. 1:11).

1. *Spirit-Filled Life Bible* (Nashville, TN: Thomas Nelson Publishers, 1991), 1878, "Word Wealth: 6:12 patience."

2. Donald Gee, *The Fruit of the Spirit* (Springfield, MO: Gospel Publishing House, 1975), 39.

3. *Spirit-Filled Life Bible,* 1780, "Word Wealth: 5:22 kindness."

4. Ibid., 1713, "Word Wealth: 15:14 goodness."

Lesson 6/ Faithfulness, Gentleness, and Self-Control

Coming to the final triad in the list of the fruit, we encounter some of the most challenging aspects of life—faithfulness, gentleness, and self-control. We live in a society in which people are becoming increasingly untrustworthy; even within the confines of church leadership we wonder, "Where's the integrity? the trustworthiness?" And what about marriages in which one or both spouses lack loyalty? Yet, trustworthiness and loyalty are what the fruit of *faithfulness* is all about.

And then there's *gentleness*—having control over rage; being courteous. Don't you sense society could use a little more "rage control" and courtesy? Physical abuse is on the rise in many homes; fits of anger regularly lead to needless killings. As for courtesy—it's almost gone! Even those in the service industry often make customers feel as if they're doing them a favor to render their paid-for service!

As for *self-control,* need we say more than illicitly contracted AIDS? Again, society is increasingly saying that an "inalienable" human right is the "right" to exercise unbridled sensual passion. "Having to learn to resist temptation is emotionally and psychologically draining; it could possibly even damage one's inner psyche and stunt his/her development as a 'whole' person!" And yet the pages of ancient Scripture still scream out, "Giving all diligence, add to your faith . . . knowledge, to knowledge self-control . . . . For if these things are yours and abound, *you will be* neither barren nor unfruitful in the knowledge of our Lord Jesus Christ" (2 Pet. 1:5, 6, 8).

Ready to dive into the final triad? They may prove challenging, but they present an exciting opportunity to plunge further into the depths of His life and to become a sweet fragrance in an otherwise decaying society. People need positive role models; they need Christians who accurately reflect the life of God. They need to see "children of God without fault in the midst of a crooked and perverse generation" (Phil. 2:15). Let's give the Spirit our lives, the needed raw material to produce many King's kids who "shine as lights in the world"!

"I CAN ALWAYS COUNT ON MICHAEL!"

Wouldn't you like people to be able to put your name where Michael's is? I know I would. I particularly want God to be able to put it there. Not for reasons of works of righteousness or pride, but out of sincere gratitude for the opportunity to serve Jesus Christ, I trust someday He'll say to me, "Well *done*, good and faithful servant" (Matt. 25:23). This is what the fruit of *faithfulness* is all about.

Even society outside the church recognizes the need for faithfulness. Banks lend money anticipating the faithfulness of the payer to make the monthly payments; children anticipate the faithfulness of their parent(s) to provide food, clothing and lodging for them; governments anticipate the faithfulness of foreign powers in maintaining treaties. Where there is a lack of faithfulness, there is confusion and chaos. How much more so the need for faithfulness in God's church, built on Christ Jesus Himself, "the Amen, the Faithful and True Witness" (Rev. 3:14)?

 WORD WEALTH

Faithfulness, *pistis.* *Pistis* has a wide range of meanings. It can refer to a body of truth which we believe; the basic trust which one has in God for salvation; or the dynamic power which realizes the energy contained in the promises of God. It can be translated conviction, confidence, trust, belief, faith, reliance, trustworthiness, faithfulness, or persuasion. Thus, the idea of "faithfulness" reflects a fullness and steadfastness of such trust and trustworthiness as a character trait of the believer.

In lists of practical ethical responsibilities, as in this text, the focus is on one's *reliability*. Because God is faithfully dependable, the Holy Spirit is able to develop dependability in God's people. The statement regarding the early apostles and their colleagues undoubtedly holds true for all Christians: "It is required in stewards that one be found faithful" (1 Cor. 4:2).

THE MODEL OF GOD

Read the following New Testament passages and note what is attributed to God's faithfulness.

1 Cor. 1:9

1 Cor. 10:13

1 Thess. 5:23, 24

2 Thess. 3:3

1 John 1:9

THE PARABLE OF THE TALENTS

The parable of the talents in Matthew 25:14–30 ties together readiness for Jesus' return with responsible activity. Carefully read the passage and note the following about faithfulness:

"Talents" here represent privileges and opportunities given us to serve the purposes of the kingdom of God. According to verse 15, how are such opportunities distributed to us?

According to verses 16, 17, what is expected of us if we're to be deemed faithful, responsible kingdom workers?

According to verses 18 and 24–27, what constitutes a lack of faithfulness to the Master's work?

 FAITH ALIVE

In light of the above parable, how would you evaluate your direct involvement in kingdom purposes? Are you praying for more opportunities to faithfully serve? Are you being faithfully responsible to the duties you currently have? Discuss these issues with God and some trusted friends; set some further goals and a time frame in which to possibly fulfill them as the Spirit increases your faithfulness.

REAL, LIVE EXAMPLES

Each of the following persons is a biblical example of faithfulness. Read these passages and note how their faithfulness was demonstrated.

Moses (Heb. 3:1–6)

Epaphras (Col. 1:7, 8; 4:12)

Onesimus (Col. 4:9; Philem. 11–13)

In 2 Timothy 2:2 Paul gives a command to pastors if they want to best invest themselves in people. What is that command?

According to Revelation 2:10, to what extent should we be willing to be faithful?

"BE ANGRY, AND DO NOT SIN"

Fulfilling the above command from Ephesians 4:26 is not an easy matter. It's obviously a fruit of the Spirit! The Bible does not teach that we're never to become indignant; it instead addresses drawing the line between what might be called "righteous" and "unrighteous" anger and between controlled and uncontrolled expressions of such.

Jesus is said to be "gentle and lowly in heart" (Matt. 11:29); yet, at one point the hardness of the people's hearts caused Him such grief He "looked around at them with anger" (Mark 3:5). It is also noted that "when He had made a whip of cords, He drove them all out of the temple" (John 2:15). Anger under the Spirit's control; this is a major part of what *gentleness* is all about.

 WORD WEALTH

Gentleness, *praotes.* A disposition that is even-tempered, tranquil, balanced in spirit, unpretentious, and that has the passions under control. The word is best translated "meekness," not as an indication of weakness, but of power and strength under control. The person who possesses this quality pardons injuries, corrects faults, and rules his own spirit well.[1]

Praotes is derived from an ancient Gothic root meaning "to love." A social virtue of high value, it was popular in ancient Greek culture and philosophy. Aristotle saw *praotes* as that happy medium between passion and no feeling at all.

WHAT CAN WE LEARN?

Moses is described as being "very humble" (or "gentle," Num. 12:3). What kind of response did this enable him to display when faced with undeserved criticism? (Num. 12:1–16, especially v. 13)

How did Moses display this "gentle humbleness" when confronted with Israel's sin with the golden calf? (Ex. 32:15–20)

According to Matthew 5:5, who alone will receive ultimate vindication on the Day of Judgment and find rulership in the consummated kingdom of God?

According to 1 Peter 3:4, what gives a godly woman "incorruptible beauty"?

According to 1 Peter 3:15, what manner is necessary to properly witness to unbelievers, especially those hostile to the gospel?

According to James 1:21, what attitude is necessary to effectively have God's word implanted in our hearts?

According to Galatians 6:1, what practice is a sign of spiritual maturity in helping people overcome besetting sin?

According to 2 Timothy 2:24, 25, how should a church leader go about dealing with those who oppose the truth of the gospel?

According to Titus 3:1, 2, what is to be our overall attitude toward people with whom we live, especially "rulers and authorities"?

It becomes rather clear, therefore, that *gentleness* is not a personality type; rather, it is a heart attitude that controls our disposition toward others. In the James 1:21 passage, it stands in direct contrast to the "bitter envy and self-seeking" of James 3:14, demonstrating a willing submission to God and His word. In the Matthean, Petrine, and Pauline passages, it connotes consideration toward others, especially in terms of controlling one's anger.

"IT'S MY RIGHT AS A FREE HUMAN BEING!"

We've undoubtedly heard the above many times. Maybe we've even said it ourselves! The works of the flesh listed in opposition to the fruit of the Spirit in Galatians 5 make it obvious that mankind in general does not want to bridle his passions—especially his sexual ones. This is where *self-control* enters the picture. The final fruit of the Spirit has to do with controlling our sensual passions. It doesn't have to do with denying them through false asceticism; rather, it's bringing God-given passions under His domain and control rather than that of the flesh or the devil.

WORD WEALTH

Self-control, *enkrateia. Enkrateia* was used by the ancient Stoics to define the person who's able to morally restrain himself when tempted by evil pleasures, so as to maintain his ethical freedom. In the New Testament it refers to allowing the Holy Spirit to empower a person so that he/she is able to voluntarily abstain from anything (especially out-of-control sexual passion) which might hinder ultimately fulfilling his/her divinely appointed task. It stands in Galatians 5:23 in contrast to the gross sins of verses 19–21.

SELF-CONTROL AND THE REALITIES OF LIFE

What can we learn about self-control and evangelism from Acts 24:24–26?

What can we learn from 1 Corinthians 9:24–27 about the place of self-control in our overall spiritual growth?

What place does Paul assign self-control in Titus 1:7–9?

PROBING THE DEPTHS

A major stumbling block to the integrity of biblical self-control is the religious tendency to associate it with false asceticism or pharisaical righteousness. How does Paul address this false view in Colossians 2:16–23, and what does he propose as the proper route to biblical self-control?

CONCLUSION TO GALATIANS 5:16–26

Paul's list of "the works of the flesh" and his list of "the fruit of the Spirit" are examples of his major premise: "The flesh lusts against the Spirit, and the Spirit against the flesh; and these are contrary to one another, so that you do not do the things that you wish" (v. 17). The list of vices emphasizes self-centeredness and egocentricity; the list of virtues emphasizes Paul's earlier command: "Through love serve one another" (v. 13). As such, each of the fruit finds its Model in Jesus Christ who "did not come to be served, but to serve, and to give His life a ransom for many" (Mark 10:45).

The conclusion is therefore clear: with Christ our Model and the Holy Spirit the Source of our enablement, "let us . . . walk in the Spirit" (Gal. 5:25). Are you a candidate?

---

1. *Spirit-Filled Life Bible* (Nashville, TN: Thomas Nelson Publishers, 1991), 1847, "Word Wealth: 6:11 gentleness."

Lesson 7/Agreeing to Disagree!

Unity in the body of Christ does not mean uniformity. Though most of us are opting for a fulfillment of Jesus' prayer that "they may be one just as We are one" (John 17:22), we know this does not mean we will necessarily perceive all matters of doctrine the same. For example, a reading of three or four commentaries on the Book of Revelation will certainly convince us of this! There will doubtless always remain some areas of doctrine and practice on which we will need to "agree to disagree"! We already noted this in our previous study on Holy Spirit fullness; we'll now note it again, for categorizing the New Testament gifts is another such area of differing insights among scholars.

The New Testament gifts are found primarily in Romans, 1 Corinthians, Ephesians, and 1 Peter. In these four books, there are six different lists giving a total of thirty-seven gifts. What are we to make of the lists in these different books? To what degree do these treasures overlap? Are the gifts in Romans the same as those in 1 Corinthians? For example, when Romans 12:6 talks about "prophecy," is it the same gift as "prophecy" in 1 Corinthians 12:10? This is that with which our current study will grapple.

As noted above, there are several ways to classify the gifts; we'll study but one—namely, the view that each member of the Godhead gives gifts, and those gifts differ, though they may bear the same New Testament name. "It is important that we not blur the distinction between the gifts given by each member of the Godhead."[1]

And what about "gift mixes," that is, having a gift from each of the books? Is this possible? For example, can an Ephesians 4:11 teacher also be a Romans 12:6 prophet, or can an evangelist (Eph. 4:11) be one who shows mercy (Rom. 12:8)? Why is it some of the gifts have become titles ("Pastor John"), while others don't seem to be used as titles ("Interpretation of Tongues Sally")? These are just some of the vital questions we'll look at in this lesson as we endeavor to harmonize the various gift lists. It promises to be an exciting discovery, so let's get started.

WHAT IS THIS WE'RE OPENING?

The basic understanding of the New Testament is that God's gift of salvation brings humankind union and fellowship with God through His Son, Jesus Christ (2 Cor. 5:18). This union then leads to the granting of various gifts to His children to equip them for the resulting service (Eph. 2:10). The gifts are known in Greek as *charismata*, derived from the same root as the Greek word for "grace." Hence, they are "grace gifts"—freely bestowed faculties given out of God's goodwill to make effective ministry possible.

According to Romans 12:3–5, what must our attitude be with reference to any spiritual gift we're given?

According to 1 Peter 4:10, using our gift is part of being a good _____.

According to 1 Corinthians 14:18 and 2 Corinthians 1:11, which two gifts did Paul have?

AT A GLANCE

GIFTS IN THE SCRIPTURES

Rom. 12:6–8	1 Cor. 12:8–10	1 Cor. 12:28–30	Eph. 4:11	1 Pet. 4:11
Prophecy	Word of wisdom	Apostles	Apostles	Speaking the
Ministry	Word of knowledge	Prophets	Prophets	oracles of God
Teaching	Faith	Teachers	Evangelists	Ministering
Exhortation	Gifts of healings	Miracles	Pastors	
Giving	Working of miracles	Gifts of healings,	Teachers	
Leadership	Prophecy	helps, and		
Showing	Discerning of	administrations		
mercy	spirits	Gifts of varieties		
	Tongues	of tongues		
	Interpretation of	Gifts of		
	tongues	interpretation		

WORD WEALTH

Gift, *charisma*. Related to other words derived from the root *char*. *Chara* is joy, cheerfulness, delight. *Charis* is grace, goodwill, undeserved favor. *Charisma* is a gift of grace, a free gift, divine gratuity, spiritual endowment, miraculous faculty. It is especially used to designate the gifts of the Spirit (1Cor. 12:4–10). In modern usage, a "charismatic" signifies one who either has one or more of these gifts functioning in his life, or who believes these gifts are for today's church.[2]

FIRST . . . PETER

Of the various lists, the one in 1 Peter 4 is the shortest. Written in the first century A.D. (*ca.* A.D. 60), 1 Peter addresses a group of Christians in Asia Minor who are facing persecution. He calls them to faithful living and reminds them of the hope of salvation. He says that Christians are to show the world what salvation looks like regardless of life's circumstances; a major part of this involves the release of spiritual gifts. "If anyone speaks, *let him speak* as the oracles of God. If anyone ministers, *let him do it* as with the ability which God supplies" (4:11). Part of the work God entrusts to His church is the rendering of service to fellow believers to minister "for the profit of *all*" (1 Cor. 12:7; see Lesson 3). Such service originates primarily in one's unique gifting.

Peter's remarks are brief because he's not interested so much in how the various ministries are carried out as he is that the various ministries be respected and that they function. Ministering out of our God-given giftedness, Peter notes, is a vital part of vigilant, serious living (4:7, 10).

Carefully read 1 Peter 4:7–11 and answer the following:

Contextually, to minister out of one's giftedness is part of having _____ for one another. (v. 8)

According to verse 10, who does Peter say has received a spiritual gift?

What is each of us commanded to do with the gift we're given? (v. 10)

Peter apparently takes the manifold gifts listed in Romans 12 and Ephesians 4 and summarizes them under two major categories. What are those categories? (v. 11)

Carefully read Romans 12:6–8 and 1 Corinthians 12:7–11 and list which gifts you think would be included under each major category.

What is the purpose for releasing our gift in ministry to fellow Christians? (v. 11) What does this say to you about ministry and authentic worship?

GIFTS OF THE FATHER, SON, AND HOLY SPIRIT

We stated in the opening section of this lesson that the position taken here is that each member of the Godhead gives gifts. Though the selection is somewhat lengthy, it is very important to your understanding that you read the following by Paul Walker before continuing. It will give focus to the studies that follow:

> For many, clarification of the distinct role each member of the Godhead plays in giving gifts to mankind is helpful. Foundationally, our course, our existence—human life—is given by the Father (Gen. 2:7; Heb. 12:9), who also gave His only begotten Son as the Redeemer for mankind (John 3:16). Redemptively, Jesus is the giver of eternal life (John 5:38–40; 10:27, 28); He gave His life and shed His blood to gain that privilege (John 10:17, 18; Eph. 5:25–27). Further, the Father and Son have jointly sent the Holy Spirit (Acts 2:17, 33) to advance the work of redemption through the church's ministry of worship, growth, and evangelism.
>
> In sequence, then, we find Romans 12:3–8 describing gifts given by God as Father. They seem to characterize basic "motivations," that is, inherent tendencies that characterize each different person by reason of the Creator's unique workmanship in their initial gifting. . . .
>
> Second, in 1 Corinthians 12:7–11, the nine gifts of the Holy Spirit are listed. Their purpose is specific—to "profit" the body of the church. . . . These nine gifts are specifically available to *every* believer as the Holy Spirit distributes them (1 Cor. 12:11). They

are not to be merely acknowledged in a passive way, but rather are to be actively welcomed and expected (1 Cor. 13:1; 14:1).

Third, the gifts which the Son of God has given are pivotal in assuring that the first two categories of gifts are applied in the body of the church. Ephesians 4:7–16 indicates the "office gifts" Christ has placed in the church along with their purpose. . . .

In this light, we examine these clearly designated categories of giftings: the Father's (Rom. 12:6–8), the Son's (Eph. 4:11) and the Holy Spirit's (1 Cor. 12:8–10).[3]

THE FATHER'S PURPOSE
(Romans 12:1–8)

Carefully read the above passage and note the following:

What is the overall purpose in this section? (v. 1)

This purpose in part calls for a _____ of our minds (v. 2).

What is the purpose of this renewal? (v. 2)

According to verse 3, to determine one's spiritual gift and to keep from having an over-inflated view of oneself requires what kind of thinking?

According to verse 6, what does God intend to be done with these gifts?

According to verse 3, what is another way to term the gifts listed here?

This listing of gifts then refers to those bestowed by the Father (cf. 1 Cor. 12:4–6) and are frequently termed "Creational Gifts." They have to do with a person's basic inward driving motivation or perspective on life. This will be more completely explained in Lesson 8.

 WORD WEALTH

Soberly, *sophroneo. Sophroneo* can mean to observe proper moderation or exercise self-control. Some English versions translate it "with sober judgment." It is used in Mark 5:15 to describe the delivered Gadarene demoniac ("clothed and in his <u>right mind</u>"); in Titus 2:6 Titus is told to "exhort the young men to be <u>sober-minded.</u>" It is an antonym to one's thinking *"of himself* more highly than he ought to think" (Rom. 12:3).

"Because the Bible teaches that human beings are made in God's image, we are to respect the position of each individual under God. This text does not teach that believers should think of themselves as worthless or insignificant beings, but rather that none should consider himself to be more worthy, more important, more deserving of salvation, or more essential than anyone else. Possession of different talents or gifts does not denote differences in worth, for all belong to the one body, to one another, and all are interdependent (vv. 4, 5). To think otherwise is to distort reality. Each individual has intrinsic value and worth, as we are all equal before God and in Christ."[4]

THE SON'S PURPOSE
(Ephesians 4:1–16)

Ephesians deals with the nature of the church. It's unique among Paul's writings because it deals with the church as the universal body of Christ (Eph. 1:23) rather than the church as a local congregation. It also presents God's plan for the ages and how the church is part of that plan. As such, the gifts listed in 4:11 are timeless gifts to the church universal which are to find their outworking in and through local congregations, all in the eternal purposes of God. Even Paul, an apostle, was anchored to the church at Antioch (Acts 13:1) and returned there whenever his itinerary allowed.

These particular gifts are clearly those "given according to the measure of Christ's gift" (v. 7). Carefully read Ephesians 4:1–16 and answer the following:

According to verse 8, what precipitated the giving of the gifts listed in verse 11?

List the specific "office gifts" in verse 11.

What is the purpose of giving these gifts? (v. 12a)

What is the purpose of equipping the saints? (v. 12b)

According to verse 13, how long does God intend to use this plan outlined in verses 11 and 12?

According to verse 16, what transpires when properly equipped saints become part of a local church and effectively do the work of ministry?

"The 'work of ministry' is the enterprise of each member of the body of Christ and not the exclusive charge of select leaders. . . . The task of the gifted leader is to cultivate the individual and corporate ministries of those he or she leads. . . .

A progress in maturity (v. 13), stability (v. 14), and integrity (v. 15), taking place in every individual member's experience, results in the whole body's growth (numerical expansion) and edifying (internal strengthening)."[5]

THE SPIRIT'S PURPOSE
(1 Corinthians 12:4–11)

Corinth was a very important commercial city of the day. Paul had founded the church there about A.D. 50–51. This letter was sent to deal with certain doctrinal and practical problems in the relatively young congregation. As former pagans, the Corinthians shifted some of their pagan practices and beliefs over to their walk with the Holy Spirit. It is in correcting this error that Paul deals with the matter of the gifts of the Spirit. Each gift is clearly designated as a "manifestation of the Spirit" (v. 7).

What do you notice in verses 4–6 that substantiates our view that the New Testament speaks of three categories of gifts corresponding to each member of the Trinity?

"The three categories named in these verses coupled with the Trinity show the broad diversity, yet essential unity, in the manifestation of the Spirit. Unity does not make the Spirit uniform. The Holy Spirit is not an impersonal power, and His gifts do not spring from a human source; it is the work of God. Gifts are from the great gift, the Holy Spirit; ministries are modeled by the main minister, Christ (the Lord); and the works of the Spirit come from the chief worker, God the Father."[6]

List the nine manifestations noted in verses 8–10.

According to verse 11, to whom are these manifestations given? How is their giving determined?

WORD WEALTH

Manifestation, *phanerosis. Phanerosis* means disclosure or announcement. It represents in 1 Corinthians visible evidence of the Spirit's activity. The basic Greek root *phan* is the same as that for an apparition or ghost. Hence, it can have overtones of a disclosure that sort of "flashes forth." It is used in context as a synonym for "gift," but with the apparent nuance that these nine aspects can "flash forth from any believer as needed" ("for the profit *of all*"). Hence, they are not inherent heightened abilities, as the basic Romans 12 gifts nor ecclesiastical functions/titles as Ephesians 4 gifts. Understanding such distinctions "prevents us from confusing our foundational motivation in life and service for God with our purposeful quest for an openness to His Holy Spirit's full resources and power for service and ministry."[7]

FAITH ALIVE

Can you identify your Romans 12 gift? How about those of you who feel called to "full-time" ministry—do you sense you have an Ephesians 4:11 gift? If so, which one? How open are you to being used in various manifestations of the Spirit? Are you earnestly seeking to be used in them?

First Timothy 3:10 says gifting in our lives needs to be documented by responsible leadership in a local church who see it operating. Do you have such a group around you? Do their perceptions agree with your own?

How's your "ego" doing with reference to gifted ministry? Is your self-estimation healthy, as outlined in Romans 12? Carefully consider all these questions in prayer and, again, so far as is possible, have someone praying with you and helping hold you accountable.

1. *Spirit-Filled Life Bible* (Nashville, TN: Thomas Nelson Publishers, 1991), 1737, "Kingdom Dynamics: The Holy Spirit's Gifts to You."
2. Ibid., 1719, "Word Wealth: 1:7 gift."
3. Ibid., 2022–2023, "Kingdom Dynamics: Holy Spirit Gifts and Power."
4. Ibid., 1708, "Kingdom Dynamics: One Should Not Think Too Highly of Himself."
5. Ibid., 1793, notes on 4:12 and 4:13–16.
6. Ibid., 1736, note on 12:4–6.
7. Ibid., 2023, "Kingdom Dynamics: Holy Spirit Gifts and Power."

Lesson 8/The Creational Gifts

This is a study of Romans 12:3–8. We have established that the Romans 12 gifts are the gifts of the Father, commonly referred to as "Creational Gifts." They have to do with our basic inward driving bent in life. A proper understanding of this passage and its gifts can truly transform our image of ourselves, for so much of our self-image is tied into understanding how God has "wired" us. "Why do I always just seem to want to give?" "Why am I so tuned in with people's emotions?" "Why do I always want to see to it that people 'learn their lessons' and 'play by the rules'?" "Why aren't I as good an organizer as Brother Tom?" This is what understanding Creational Gifts is all about.

The unfortunate dilemma facing many is that they feel they are of no special value. Many believers feel that any "moron" could easily take their place in life and in the church. This is tragic, for God does not create "morons." Each life is unique to God, and His intent is that each person live out that very special and precious uniqueness (Ps. 139:13–18; Jer. 1:5). It is not His intention that people go through life endlessly searching for their place in society or the church, constantly in turmoil in their spirit as to who they are—jumping from career to career or ministry to ministry to try to find themselves.

Nor is it God's intent that anyone in His body feel that he/she is the only one or best one in the body because of a particular gift. Born out of a misunderstanding of God's intended design for His church, this pride can be as sinful a tendency as having a low self-image. Remember what we established in the last lesson about thinking soberly? We need to keep this in mind as we study each of these gifts, "For as we have many members in one body, but all the members do not have the same function, so we, *being* many, are one body in Christ, and individually members of one another" (Rom. 12:4, 5). There is no hierarchy with these gifts; our tendency is to opt to have what we deem to be the more "glamorous" gifts, such as prophecy or teaching; but God knows no such hierarchical distinction. Each person is vital as is each gift.

So let's progress, seeing what we can discover about each of these gifts.

A MEASURE OF FAITH

"God has dealt to each one a measure of faith" (v. 3). "Has dealt" has the idea of being divided out. "Measure of faith" refers not to "saving faith but the faith to receive and exercise the gifts God apportions to us."[1] Paul then uses "has dealt to each one a measure of faith" interchangeably with "having . . . gifts differing according to the grace that is given to us" (v. 6).

Read Romans 12:6–8 and list the gifts.

Reread these verses and note the specific command that accompanies each gift.

PROPHECY

"If prophecy, *let us prophesy* in proportion to our faith" (v. 6).

WORD WEALTH

Prophecies, *propheteia.* From *pro,* "forth," and *phemi,* "to speak." The primary use of the word is not predictive, in the sense of foretelling, but interpretive, declaring, or forth-telling the will and counsel of God.[2] It has to do with becoming aware of God's undisclosed truths and proclaiming them as they are disclosed. Tremendous spiritual perception accompanies prophetic utterance. On occasion in the Old Testament a person with prophetic insight was called a "seer" (1 Sam. 9:18; 2 Chr. 33:18).

Prophecy in the Bible is very diverse. It can function all the way from the arch-Prophet, Jesus Christ, to the Old Testament classical prophets, to ongoing prophetic ministries in the church, to a Creational Gift, to a manifestation of the Spirit. Therefore, the precise understanding of prophecy, especially in the gift lists, is determined according to the overall context of the list. Therefore, a person with the Romans 12:6 gift of prophecy would be a person endowed by God with an exceptional ability to perceive matters, not based on any ministry office or particular manifestation of the Spirit. He/she sees all of life with special prophetic insight. Some have therefore renamed this particular Creational Gift "insight" to distinguish it from the Ephesians 4:11 and 1 Corinthians 12:10 gifts. Such is linguistically and contextually legitimate.

First Corinthians 14:24, 25, though talking about the manifestation of the Spirit gift of prophecy, gives valuable information about the nature of prophecy in general that is transferable to this gift as well. Read that section and answer the following:

According to verse 24, what two things does prophecy do?

According to verses 24, 25a, what is the relationship between prophetic insight and secret intents or motives of the heart?

What is the result of this prophetic disclosure? (v. 25b)

Because no gift operates in perfection without interven-
tion from the flesh, what is Paul's warning attached to this
gift? (v. 26)

From your understanding of this gift, what special application do you think Colossians 3:12, 13 might have in the lives
of those with this particular gift?

A person with this gift then will view all of life with a
desire to see conviction, accountability, repentance, confession
and a keen awareness of God brought into focus. He/she will
hardly be able to function around others without these aspects
of God's life churning deep within. There is a deep concern
that motives be right and that people face up to the truth
about themselves, clearly understanding the realities behind
what they are doing. This is why this gift must be exercised
with humility and with an ear close to God.

MINISTRY

"Or ministry, *let us use it* in *our* ministering" (Rom. 12: 7).

 **WORD WEALTH**

Ministry, *diakonia. Diakonia* occurs some thirty-four
times in the New Testament. Its basic meaning is "rendering
personal help, aid or assistance to others." In secular Greek it
was used for the activity of waiting on tables, caring for
household needs or serving in general. It is from the same
Greek root as the word for "deacon" (1 Tim. 3:8).

How did those from "the household of Stephanas" minister? (1 Cor. 16:15)

Using Jesus as our Model, what is to be the attitude of those with this gift? (Matt. 20:28)

A LOOK AT MARTHA

According to John 12:2, what is one way Martha is remembered?

According to Luke 10:38, what is one way those with this gift demonstrate it?

According to Luke 10:39, 40, what seems to be the preference of those with this gift?

According to Luke 10:40, what seems to be a possible liability associated with this gift?

According to the exhortation accompanying this gift in Romans 12:7, what seems to be another possible liability associated with this gift?

Those with the gift of ministry, then, are graced in a special way to show God's love by meeting practical needs and rendering assistance. They are sometimes called "servers" and find great satisfaction in doing things for others. They are the "hands and feet" of the body of Christ in an extraordinary way, often preferring doing something with their hands over speaking. They see to it that the body of Christ has its practical needs met and that jobs within the church get done well and efficiently. Although this gift is not tied into any specific church office, a person with the gift makes an excellent deacon or deaconess.

HE WHO TEACHES

"He who teaches, in teaching" (Rom. 12:7).

WORD WEALTH

Teach, *didasko.* In classical Greek the root meaning of *didasko* suggested the idea of causing someone to accept something. It can be translated "to teach, inform, instruct, demonstrate or prescribe." It has as its aim that of systematically communicating knowledge and skill so as to develop people. Teachers give themselves to facts and systematic instruction. In the New Testament the focus of teaching is how to live out God's will.

People with this Romans 12:7 gift are those who, regardless of their office or particular ministry in the body of Christ, are motivated by a desire to clarify and expound truth. They enjoy mental challenges and learning. They are generally able to communicate well and will always have a driving need for biblical truth to be accurately expounded with well-documented proof of any conclusions drawn.

In what sense of the word *teach* might it be an activity true of all believers? (Col. 3:16)

What exhortation is given those with this gift? (Rom. 12:7) What might this indicate about those with this gift speaking up and releasing it?

From Jesus, the Great Teacher, we learn many truths about teaching in general that apply to this gift as well.

What was the essential source of ability for Jesus' teachings? (Luke 4:17)

What were His two primary objectives in teaching? (Matt. 22:34–40)

On at least one occasion, to what did He ascribe greatness in the kingdom of God? (Matt. 5:19, 20)

Again, these teachers may or may not teach formally in the church, but they press us on every hand to understand sound doctrine and to be properly taught in the Word.

HE WHO EXHORTS

"He who exhorts, in exhortation" (Rom. 12:8).

 **WORD WEALTH**

Exhort, *parakaleo.* A calling alongside to help, to comfort, to give consolation or encouragement, to appeal to, to urge or to cheer up; an exhorter offers a strengthening presence and upholds those appealing for assistance while urging them to pursue a certain course of conduct. *Paraklesis* ("exhortation") can come to us by the Holy Spirit, by the Scriptures or by other people with this gift (2 Cor. 5:20). (See also **Helper** in Lesson 1.)

Someone with this particular Romans 12 gift is motivated to see people encouraged toward growth in the Lord. They are equipped with the special grace of stimulating or guiding people (cf. Acts 8:31) to worthy conduct and personal progress; they make doctrine practical. They tend to be very positive people with a basically positive outlook on life. They are always interested in seeing how tribulation or adversity can be turned into successful living and maturity in the Lord.

According to 1 Thessalonians 2:11, 12 and 4:9, 10, what are some specific areas in which exhorters are interested in seeing growth and success?

According to Acts 14:22, what is another area?

We're told in Acts 4:36 that one "Joses . . . was also named Barnabas by the apostles (which is translated Son of Encouragement)." What do we learn from his life about those with the gift of exhortation?

Acts 9:27

Acts 15:39 with Col. 4:10

Exhorters make very effective preachers; but, again, these gifts are independent of ecclesiastical office.

HE WHO GIVES

"He who gives, with liberality" (Rom. 12:8).

WORD WEALTH

Gives, *metadidomi.* To give, share, impart, distribute, grant. The word implies liberality or generosity. It is used to exhort those with two outer tunics to give one to someone who has none (Luke 3:11); to encourage people to give with cheerful outflow (Rom. 12:8); and to urge workers to labor with industry in order to give to him who has a need (Eph. 4:28). It also has the idea of supporting or spending yourself for someone else.

Those with this Romans 12 gift are not just financial givers; they are more overall contributors with a grace gift to give material, physical, emotional, and psychological support to others. They are special sharers, sharing of themselves to lend supportive encouragement to people. They stand with and undergird people and projects; their chief desire is to make sure people are supported.

Read the following passages and note what is to be shared or imparted to others through this gift.

Luke 3:11

Rom. 1:11

Eph. 4:28

1 Thess. 2:8

A LOOK AT ABRAHAM

Abraham models the gift of giving. Since he was a real contributor, let's look at his life.

What does Genesis 13:2 say about his being entrusted with assets?

What does Genesis 14:11–16 say about his willingness to act on behalf of others in need?

What does Genesis 14:17–20 say about his attitude toward tithing?

What does Genesis 22:1–3 say about his willingness to give sacrificially?

What does Genesis 23:1–16 say about his awareness of the value of things and a desire to be honest with a purchase?

Those who give, then, see to it that we have access to sufficient assets and receive supportive encouragement to get things done for Christ. They're exhorted to give "with liberality." The word has the idea of being liberal, generous, and free-flowing. In other words, those with this gift must watch the temptation to give selfishly or to give hoping to get something back or expecting others to do the same.

HE WHO LEADS

"He who leads, with diligence" (Rom. 12:8).

 WORD WEALTH

Leads, *prohistemi. Prohistemi* means to be at the head of, to rule, to direct, to manage or to give leadership aid. It was often used for people in the position of superintendence or those who were leaders in an army, a state or a political party. Another word might be "facilitators."

These Romans 12:8 people are gifted to coordinate people to carry out activities and goals. They are particularly gifted at sensing overall problems, surveying needs, enlisting others to do work, assessing the time needed to complete a goal, organizing resources, proceeding under opposition and pressure and delegating authority. They provide the necessary ingredient for God's people to effectively organize and carry out their goals.

In 1 Thessalonians 5:12 this word describes those who do what?

In 1 Timothy 3:4 it describes an elder's management of what?

How is one to lead? (Rom. 12:8)

"Diligence" has the idea of striving for, being zealous for, or industriously seeking to do something (2 Tim. 2:15; 4:9).

Nehemiah exercised this gift of leadership with diligence. Read the following passages in Nehemiah to gain further understanding into the nature of this gift: 1:3, 4; 2:6,
12–18; 3; 4; 5:1–19; 7:1, 2.

HE WHO SHOWS MERCY

"He who shows mercy, with cheerfulness" (Rom. 12:8).

    WORD WEALTH

Mercy, *eleeo.* *Eleeo* means to have mercy or pity on
someone, to be merciful or compassionate or to help someone out of pity. In classical Greek it often described the emotions felt by contact with an affliction that came undeservedly
on someone.

These Romans 12 people are those whom God has
endowed with a special measure of faith to emotionally identify
with people so as to show compassion. They are strong "feel-
ers," with a marked ability to perceive where people are emotionally and to identify with what they are feeling or going
through. They aim at doing good and helping others through
the motivation of empathy. They shun hard-heartedness;
they're the "heart" of the church in a special way.

According to Mark 5:19, why was the demoniac at Gerasa
delivered?

According to Matthew 23:23, mercy is regarded as what?

According to James 3:17, mercy is a sign of what?

According to Romans 12:8, how is this mercy to be extended?

"Cheerfulness" means gladness or graciousness; it's being a sunbeam of light in a sickroom. The exhortation to cheerfulness likely accompanies the gift of mercy because the strong feeling base of the gift makes it subject to moroseness or emotional depression.

THE GOOD SAMARITAN

Read Luke 10:29–37 and note the following about the gift of mercy in action.

How did the Samaritan respond to the victim's distress? (v. 33)

What did he do to help? (v. 34)

How was he willing to involve himself? (v. 35)

CONCLUSION

"While only seven categories [of gifts] are listed, observation indicates that few people are fully described by only one. More commonly a mix is found, with different traits of each gift present to some degree, while usually one will be the dominant trait of that person. It would be a mistake to suppose that an individual's learning to respond to the Creator's gifting of them in one or more of these categories fulfills the Bible's call to 'earnestly desire the best gifts' (1 Cor. 12:31). These gifts of our place in God's created order are foundational."[3] Therefore, in addition to our Romans 12 gift(s) each of us will be used in various manifestations of the Spirit as He chooses (1 Cor. 12); some of us will also have an Ephesians 4:11 gift or the gift of helps, administrations or deacon/deaconness.

 FAITH ALIVE

Discovering your Romans 12 gift(s) is vitally important. Pray over this material carefully to see where you might fit. For additional information you might check the resource "Motivational Gifts" from The Cutting Edge, 2218 Roberts Road, Medford, OR 97504; (503) 772-9502.

1. *Spirit-Filled Life Bible* (Nashville, TN: Thomas Nelson Publishers, 1991), 1708, note on 12:3.
2. Ibid., 1831, "Word Wealth: 5:20 prophecies."
3. Ibid., 2023, "Kingdom Dynamics: Holy Spirit Gifts and Power."

Lesson 9/Office Gifts

This is a study of Ephesians 4:1–16 and the so-called "Office Gifts" of Christ Himself to the church: "He Himself gave some *to be* apostles, some prophets, some evangelists, and some pastors and teachers" (v. 11). Evangelists, pastors and teachers are perhaps the best known and most universally accepted of all the gifts in the church. A couple of these gifts are even common titles: "Evangelist John Smith" or "Pastor Robert Jones." In many ecclesiastical circles, apostles and prophets are a different matter, but we'll save understanding these gifts for our upcoming study!

The Book of Ephesians is largely about the church. It deals with how God is bringing the church to her intended place in His kingdom. It is generally agreed that Ephesians falls into two sections, with chapter 4 heading up the second section. Having established the Christian's position in Christ and the truth that Christ has only one church (chs. 1—3), Paul moves into practical exhortations of daily Christian life-style (chs. 4—6). "Walk worthy of the calling with which you were called . . . endeavoring to keep the unity of the Spirit in the bond of peace" (4:1, 3). Doing so obviously requires great maturity, a maturity enhanced and strengthened as the various 4:11 gifts give themselves to "the equipping of the saints for the work of ministry, for the edifying of the body of Christ" (v. 12).

The Model for each of the gifts is again Jesus Himself. He's the "Apostle . . . of our confession" (Heb. 3:1), "a Prophet" like Moses (Acts 3:22), an evangelist "anointed . . . to preach the gospel" (Luke 4:18, 19), "the Shepherd . . . of your souls" (1 Pet. 2:25) and the "Teacher" (John 13:13). As the Model, He intends His multifaceted ministry to be carried on in the church by the various Office Gifts. They are invaluable to the kingdom of God. We need, therefore, to truly understand and appreciate these gifts, as well as the tasks to which they're called.

Let's proceed then with an open mind and heart. Some of what we explore may be new or even contrary to some of your church tradition. But let's give Scripture a fresh and fair chance to speak for itself; we just may be surprised at what we discover!

THE UNITY AND PURPOSE OF THE CHURCH

Understanding the context of the Ephesians 4:11 gifts is crucial. Paul begins with an appeal to unity within the body of Christ that is the responsibility of each believer and is to be pursued earnestly.

Let's explore Ephesians 4:1–16.

What is Paul's appeal? (v. 1)

What is to be the attitude with which we are to carry out this appeal? (v. 2)

What should be a key desire of our hearts? (v. 3)

Why should we be "endeavoring to keep the unity of the Spirit in the bond of peace"? (vv. 4–6)

Unity does not rule out diversity. Although there is but "one body," what is true within that one body? (v. 7)

What did Christ have to do to make the gifts in verse 11 available to humankind? (vv. 8–10)

◧ BEHIND THE SCENES

There is great diversity of opinion among scholars as to the meaning of Paul's parenthetical thought in verses 9, 10. "Christ's descent into the lower parts of the earth has been variously interpreted as a descent into hell (associating it with 1 Pet. 3:19), a descent into Sheol/Hades (the realm of the dead [see Acts 2:25–35]), or as symbolically referring to His incarnation (whereby Christ descended to Earth from heaven), a descent carrying Him to the depths of humiliation (see Phil. 2:5–11)."[1] Using two or three reputable commentaries on Ephesians, research these verses to see the basis for the various arguments. Of particular value to those with some background in New Testament Greek is *Word Biblical Commentary, Volume 42—Ephesians,* by Andrew Lincoln (Dallas, TX: Word Books, 1990); for non-Greek students, see *The Letter of Paul to the Ephesians,* rev. ed., by Francis Foulkes (Grand Rapids, MI: William B. Eerdmans Publishing Company, 1989).

What is the purpose of the Ephesians 4:11 gifts? (v. 12a)

What is the purpose of "the equipping of the saints"? (v. 12b)

 WORD WEALTH

Equipping, *katartismos.* A making fit, preparing, training, perfecting, making fully qualified for service. In classical language the word is used for setting a bone during surgery.

The Great Physician is now making all the necessary adjustments so the church will not be "out of joint."[2]

According to verse 13, how long does God intend to use the plan outlined in verses 11 and 12?

According to verse 14, what is the purpose of our coming "to the measure of the stature of the fullness of Christ"? (v. 13)

According to verse 16, equipped saints fully functioning in a local church in "the work of ministry" (v. 12) is necessary for what?

"SOME TO BE APOSTLES"

 WORD WEALTH

Apostles, *apostolos.* A special messenger, a delegate, one commissioned for a particular task or role, one who is sent forth with a message. In the New Testament the word denotes both the original twelve disciples and prominent leaders outside the Twelve. Marvin Vincent records three features of an apostle: 1) one who has had a visible encounter with the resurrected Christ; 2) one who plants churches; 3) one who functions in the ministry with signs, wonders, and miracles.[3]
It is important from the start to distinguish between the founding apostles (Eph. 2:20; Rev. 21:14) and the office apostles mentioned here. To be a founding apostle meant a visible encounter with the resurrected Christ as well as a key revelational/authoritative role in establishing the church, including, in some cases, writing Scripture. "Beyond the distinct role filled by the original founding apostles . . . the New Testament mentions enough additional apostles to indicate that this office, with that of prophets, is as continuing a ministry in the church as the more commonly acknowledged

offices of evangelists, pastors, and teachers (some make pastor-teacher one office)."[4] This insight is also substantiated by the fact discovered above—namely, God plans to use all five ministries in verse 11 "till we all come to the unity of the faith" (v. 13).

KEY ASPECTS OF APOSTLES

Read John 7:14–18 and note from Jesus' life three key aspects of apostleship.

Who ultimately commissions apostles? (v. 16)

In whose authority do apostles speak? (v. 17) What happens if this authority is violated? (v. 18)

What is an apostle's chief ministry responsibility? (v. 16; cf. also Mark 3:14, 15)

BARNABAS
An Apostle Outside the Twelve (Acts 14:14)

Read the following and note some personal qualities in Barnabas's apostolic life:

Acts 4:33–37

Acts 11:22–24

Acts 15:25, 26

Read the following and note aspects of Barnabas's apostolic ministry:

Acts 13:1–3

Acts 14:20–23

Acts 15:35

"Apostles" in apostolic days referred to a select group chosen to carry out directly the ministry of Christ and included the assigned task given to a few to complete the sacred canon of the Holy Scriptures; it implies the exercise of a distinct representative role of broader leadership given by Christ; an apostle functions as a messenger or spokesman of God. In contemporary times it refers to those who have the spirit of apostleship in remarkably extending the work of the church, opening fields to the gospel, and overseeing larger sections of the body of Jesus Christ.[5]

"SOME PROPHETS"

WORD WEALTH

Prophet, *prophetes.* From *pro,* "forth," and *phemi,* "to speak." A prophet, therefore, is primarily a forth-teller, one who speaks forth a divine message that can at times include foretelling future events. Among the Greeks, the prophet was the interpreter of the divine will, and this idea is dominant in biblical usage. Prophets are therefore specially endowed with insights into the counsels of the Lord and serve as His spokesmen. Prophecy is a gift of the Holy Spirit (1 Cor. 12:12), which the New Testament encourages believers to exercise, although at a level different from those with the prophetic office (Eph. 4:11).[6]

As with the apostles, those in the ongoing Ephesians 4:11 office of prophet must be distinguished from the founding prophets (cf. Eph. 2:20; see also "Apostles" above). They are named among the normal New Testament ministries (1 Cor. 12:28; Acts 13:1; 15:32); they equip the saints as key spokespersons for the Spirit (cf. Amos 3:7).

NEW TESTAMENT PROPHETIC PEOPLE

Read the following and note what it says about prophetic ministry.

Luke 2:26–28

Acts 11:28

Acts 15:32

Acts 21:11

Carefully read Acts 21:7–14. What do you notice about Paul's reception of Agabus's plea that he "not . . . go up to Jerusalem"? (v. 12)

As a true prophet, what was Agabus's ultimate concern, even if it was different than he perceived? (v. 14)

See also under "Prophecy" in Lesson 8, since many of the aspects of the Romans 12 gift apply to those with the Office Gift as well. Prophets/prophecy is a very diffuse biblical gift. New Testament prophets, then, are specially graced speakers for the Spirit, making known God's will for given situations from an ongoing church leadership perspective. Though authoritative, they are not above criticism nor above taking exception with, as seen in the incident with Paul and Agabus above. They are subject to basically the same scrutiny as the manifestation of prophecy which will be examined in Lesson 13.

"SOME EVANGELISTS"

 WORD WEALTH

Evangelist, *euangelistes.* From *euangelizo,* to announce good news, especially the gospel, to declare good tidings. An evangelist is a preacher of the gospel. Evangelist occurs three times in the New Testament (Acts 21:8; Eph. 4:11; 2 Tim. 4:5); many in the early church were apparently itinerate. The message of the evangelist is naturally largely to unbelievers, unlike that of the prophet which is largely to the church. However, as noted above, part of the evangelist's function is also "for the equipping of the saints for the work of ministry." They are to keep the preaching of Christ constantly before the church while training and encouraging believers to spread the gospel message.

PHILIP THE EVANGELIST

As one of the men who originally helped with the Hellenist problem in the early church (Acts 6:1–7), Luke notes that Philip later became an Ephesians 4:11 evangelist (Acts 21:8).

What is the major content of his message? (Acts 8:5)

What accompanied his preaching? (Acts 8:6, 7)

In Acts 8:6 Philip evangelizes "the multitudes." What is he seen doing in Acts 8:27–38?

According to Acts 8:40, did Philip evangelize only when he had formally scheduled crusades?

According to Acts 8:12, how did Philip help establish his new converts?

According to Acts 21:8, 9, what can we learn about his family? Does he seem to have a home in order? Does he seem to have an established residence?

As one of the fivefold team members, the evangelist then should be inseparably linked to the local church; all evangelists should have a "home church" from which they operate and which they equip in a special ongoing way. But their field is the world. "Evangelist refers primarily to a special gift of preaching or witnessing in a way that brings unbelievers into the experience of salvation. . . . Essentially, the gift of evangelist operates to establish converts and to gather them spiritually and literally into the body of Christ."[7]

"SOME PASTORS"

WORD WEALTH

Pastor, *poimen.* A herdsman, sheepherder; one who tends, leads, guides, cherishes, feeds, and protects a flock. The New Testament uses the word for a Christian pastor to whose care and leadership others will commit themselves (Eph. 4:11). The term is applied metaphorically to Christ (John 10:11, 14, 16; Heb. 13:20; 1 Pet. 2:25).

Poimen defines the nature of the task involved; it is often used interchangeably with "bishop" which defines the responsibility of taking charge or giving oversight and/or with "elder" which defines the character of the pastor's person—a mature, experienced example.

CHRIST, THE TRUE SHEPHERD

Carefully read John 10:1–18 and note the following about a true shepherd:

He _____ and _____ his own sheep. (v. 3)

The sheep _____ him. (v. 4)

He _____ his life for his sheep. (v. 11)

According to John 21:16 and 1 Peter 5:2, what else does a true shepherd do?

The pastoral duties are multifaceted, as seen in Paul's instruction to his young disciple-pastor Timothy: "Preach the word! Be ready in season *and* out of season. Convince, rebuke, exhort, with all longsuffering and teaching" (2 Tim. 4:2).

AT A GLANCE

Timothy's Ministry (2 Tim. 4:5)[8]	
Timothy must . . .	Because . . .
Share in suffering for the gospel (1:8; 2:3)	Through such sharing others will be saved (2:10)
Continue in sound doctrine (1:13; 2:15)	False doctrine spreads and leads to ungodliness (2:16, 17)
Flee youthful lusts (2:22)	He must be cleansed and set apart for the Master's use (2:21)
Avoid contentiousness (2:23–25)	He must gently lead others to the truth (2:24–26)
Militantly preach the gospel (4:2)	Great apostasy is coming (4:3, 4)

"AND TEACHERS"

 WORD WEALTH

See "WORD WEALTH" under "HE WHO TEACHES" in Lesson 8.

There is a slight variation in the Greek grammar construction before "teachers" (the definite article ["the" in English] is missing), which has caused some scholars to claim that the last two groups are identical—"teaching pastors." Some therefore refer to the fourfold Office Gifts; others to the fivefold Office Gifts. Practically speaking, it is probably best that these two offices remain closely aligned. Those with the gift of pastoring should pay attention to developing sound teaching abilities; those with the gift of teaching should keep themselves within a pastoral environment.

APOLLOS

Although not specifically named a teacher, Luke does say of Apollos that he "taught accurately the things of the Lord" (Acts 18:25). We can no doubt then learn from him about the nature of the Ephesians 4:11 teaching gift. Read Acts 18:24–28 and note the following:

How is he described in verse 24?

What does Luke note about his understanding of the Scriptures? (v. 24)

With what attitude did he teach? (v. 25)

How did he deliver his teaching? (v. 26)

How did he respond to doctrinal correction from Aquila and Priscilla? (v. 26)

What was the nature of his refutation against false doctrine? (v. 28)

What kind of asset was he to the believers' understanding sound doctrine? (v. 27)

Teachers, then, are those with the Office Gift of extraordinary teaching of sound doctrine. They are generally able to communicate well and display a profound depth of biblical wisdom and knowledge; experience shows that whereas not all those with the Romans 12:7 Creational Gift of teacher become Ephesians 4:11 Office Gift teachers, many Ephesians 4:11 teachers have as a part of their gift-mix the Romans 12:7 gift. God the Creator is also God the Redeemer and the God who calls to ministry.

CONCLUSION

In all the ministries of the church—pastoral, prophetic, evangelistic teaching, whatever the ministry is—there should be an attitude of gentleness as seen in Christ, whose descension made possible His ascension and the giving of the gifts (Eph. 4:9, 10); of longsuffering, realizing that maturity does not come quickly to God's people; and most definitely these should be the attitude of a servant's heart. There is no room in the kingdom of God for Office Gift holders who emulate a primadonna-type attitude.

 FAITH ALIVE

If you are functioning in one of these gifts, can you say you truly understand the nature of the gift? Are you "comfortable" wearing that hat, so to speak? Though ministry is hard and oftentimes with great resistance, those in a particular office should know with assurance they're within the confines of their giftedness—for their sake and the sake of those to whom they're ministering. If you're struggling or wondering, be honest with yourself before God about the matter and be honest with a couple of mature, key people in your life to see what new focus God might bring you.

If you know you're in your area of giftedness, what have you learned from this study that might reshape some of your future ministry? Where would God have you to grow? Take these matters before Him in prayer, and ask Him to show you ways to implement development.

1. *Spirit-Filled Life Bible* (Nashville, TN: Thomas Nelson Publishers, 1991), 1792, note on 4:9, 10.

2. Ibid., 1793, "Word Wealth: 4:12 equipping."

3. Ibid., 1738, "Word Wealth: 12:38 apostles."

4. Ibid., 1792, note on 4:8, 11.

5. Ibid., 2025, "Kingdom Dynamics: Holy Spirit Gifts and Power."

6. Ibid., 1405, "Word Wealth: 2:5 prophet."

7. Ibid., 2025–2026, "Kingdom Dynamics: Holy Spirit Gifts and Power."

8. *The Wesley Bible* (Nashville, TN: Thomas Nelson Publishers, 1990),1832, "Chart: Timothy's Ministry (2 Tim. 4:5)."

Lesson 10/Why All the Fuss?

We've now arrived at our last classification of gifts—the manifestations of the Holy Spirit (1 Cor. 12:8–10). Interest in these manifestations has probably been greater in this century than in any century since the first. The Pentecostal movement at the turn of our century, and the subsequent Charismatic movement of the sixties and seventies, has brought renewed focus on these manifestations from a varied cross segment of God's church. The famed Kansas City Conference held in July, 1977, saw Catholic charismatics, Episcopalians, Baptists, Presbyterians, Lutherans, Messianic Jews, Pentecostals and those from nondenominational traditions come together to exalt Jesus' common lordship and to affirm their common commitment to the fullness of the work of the Holy Spirit, including His 1 Corinthians 12:8–10 manifestations.

As we round this final corner of spiritual gifts, there are a couple of realities to keep before us. First, in spite of common interest, there is not always common understanding. Historical Pentecostals and contemporary Charismatics are known to have some different doctrinal perspectives relative to these manifestations, just as with the matter of the baptism in the Holy Spirit (see Lesson 2). Although our study here is not intended to deal with these differences, it helps just to know they exist and to always walk in humility one with another. We want solid convictions, yes; but again, let's remember Paul's own words, "For now we see in a mirror, dimly," (1 Cor. 13:12), meaning we do not understand perfectly all matters of doctrine.

Second, we are not studying these manifestations simply for increased cerebral understanding. What we established in Lesson 3 about God's wanting us fully informed relative to spiritual manifestations still holds; we'll be giving four lessons to becoming better informed. But beyond being informed is the matter of our yielding ourselves to the Spirit for the actual working of these manifestations. It is possible to know a lot about these gifts and yet not have them in operation. There is clearly a degree of sovereignty attached to their release (1 Cor. 12:11); but there is also a dutiful call to "earnestly desire the best gifts" (12:31). This is why we're devoting so much space to their study; we're making a fuss because we're convinced these gifts play a vital role in bringing to people the fullness of kingdom life. Since these manifestations are a vital link in the chain required to carry on Jesus' basic ministry of proclaiming "the acceptable year of the LORD" (Luke 4:19), God's desire is that they abound among us. What do you say we get started—both on our journey toward understanding these gifts and our renewed commitment to yield to their release?

A QUICK REVIEW?

In Lessons 3 and 7 we looked at some key aspects of 1 Corinthians 12—14. You need to go back to those sections and review what we discovered there. The truths learned there will govern our studies.

So how did you do on the review? Here are a few key questions to "test" you.

Why did Paul have to write these three chapters in the first place?

Why was the Corinthians' being "carried away" (12:2) so potentially dangerous?

What is to be our overriding motive for wanting to be used in any manifestation of the Spirit?

Can you define the meaning of "manifestation"? What's the major difference in the nature of these manifestations and the gifts listed in Romans 12 and Ephesians 4?

BEING MORE FULLY INFORMED

We also established in Lesson 7 that each member of the Godhead gives gifts. One of our supporting texts was 1 Corinthians 12:4–6. What three words does Paul use here to describe the varied ways in which each of the Trinity take action with reference to the spiritual life and gifting of the church?

a)

b)

c)

What Paul terms "gifts" from the Spirit (v. 4) are termed _____ in verse 7. What does this tell you about the nature of these two terms?

Putting together our understanding of manifestation from Lesson 7 with Paul's instruction in 1 Corinthians14:26, when can we reasonably expect the Spirit to release these manifestations, "distributing to each one individually as He wills"? (12:11)

According to 1 Corinthians 12:13, what makes us eligible for use in any of these manifestations?

Paul states in 1 Corinthians 12:7 "the manifestation of the Spirit is given to each one for the profit *of all.*" How does he further define "for the profit *of all*" in 14:12?

In light of the overall purpose for these gifts (12:7), what is unique about the manifestation of "*different* kinds of tongues"? (1 Cor. 14:4a)

First Corinthians 14:22–25 tells us a couple of ways in which prophecy in particular benefits people. What are those ways?

These nine specific Holy Spirit manifestations ("flashes, disclosures, immediate movings, spontaneously granted aids to effective ministry") are made available to every believer to more effectively carry out kingdom ministry. No one individual will be able to get the entire job done; no one individual will manifest all the gifts. We need each other and we need all the diverse gifts. Together they aid in giving instruction ("word of wisdom, word of knowledge"), in ministering to people's needs ("faith, gifts of healings, working of miracles, prophecy, discerning of spirits") and in worshiping God ("*different* kinds of tongues, the interpretation of tongues"). They are not "resident" gifts like the Romans 12 and Ephesians 4 gifts, but rather spontaneously granted tools given as the need arises and the Spirit determines (1 Cor. 12:11). Our concern should always be the release of the gift most needed to meet the needs of individuals or groups of individuals, even if that manifestation flows through someone else.

THE KINGDOM OF GOD AND THE GIFTS

Having stated our belief that these manifestations are vital in bringing people into the fullness of kingdom life, we need to take a moment and concentrate on just what we mean by "kingdom life."

Kingdom life refers to the quality of life God's kingdom brings to individuals. "The Kingdom of God" was Jesus' central message and the focus of His ministry (cf. Mark 1:15). "Kingdom" (Greek, *basileia*) is more accurately "reign" or "royal rule." It refers to the rulership of God in our lives and circumstances, rulership afforded us through a personal relationship with Jesus Christ. We're dealing with "God's sovereign rule and the entry of the Messiah, which means an end to the rule of death and deadening human systems. . . . [It] is a spiritual reality that is in one's life, over one's affairs, and expressed through one's life, love, and service."[1]

Jesus made this focus clear from early in His ministry by applying Isaiah 61:1, 2 to His ministry (Luke 4:17–21). Read that passage and note the following from verses 18, 19.

Who made possible this ministry in Jesus' life?

How did He do it?

What six things was Jesus to do/proclaim as a result of this Holy Spirit anointing?

"The prophecy of Is. 61:1, 2 describes the deliverance of Israel from exile in Babylon in terms of the Year of Jubilee, but its ultimate fulfillment awaited the coming of the messianic age. Jesus boldly claims to be the promised Messiah, and His defined ministry here becomes the ongoing essence of the good news of the gospel of the kingdom of God. Luke later makes it clear He passed this same ministry on to the disciples (9:1, 2) and ultimately to the entire church (Acts 1:1, 2)."[2]

Read the following scriptures and note further the wholeness God's kingdom brings people; we'll see later in our lessons how the manifestations of the Spirit often tie into these dynamics.

Matt. 10:1, 8

Rom. 6:12–14

Col. 1:13, 14

Col. 1:27, 28

Heb. 2:14, 15

Why all the fuss over gifts? It should seem obvious. Wholeness beyond justification is vital, and any Christian should want to see actualized wholeness in him/herself and in the lives of others. Why not, then, avail ourselves of every tool (gift) available to get the job done? It's true you can cut a lawn with a pair of scissors, but why not use a lawn mower instead? Why unnecessarily handicap ourselves? A fully equipped person certainly gets the job done better!

 KINGDOM EXTRA

Secure a Bible dictionary and read the article on "the Kingdom of God/heaven." Then take a Bible concordance and look up six to ten passages in the Gospels that refer to "the Kingdom," and record what you discover.

Unity in Diversity

Because of the importance of this matter of diversity in the manifestations of the Spirit, we need to explore 1 Corinthians 12:12–31 more closely. "In order to press the point made in the previous paragraph, the need for diversity within unity, Paul adopts a common analogy from antiquity and applies it to the Corinthian situation. In so doing, as often happens with such rich metaphors, he also makes further points about attitudes that need correcting in Corinth."[3]

What is Paul's basic supposition? (vv. 12, 13)

What seems to be Paul's basic point in verses 15–19?

What is his conclusion thus far? (v. 20)

According to verse 21, what was an apparent problem at Corinth with reference to being used by the Spirit?

Gordon Fee points out that some people of high rank in Corinth evidently felt they could get along without certain other members of the church community. Paul compared these members who were believed to be expendable with supposedly weaker parts of the physical human body (most likely the internal organs). He made the case that just as the human body would cease to be whole and wholly functioning without all its parts, so the church would be weakened by the loss of any of its members. All serve a useful purpose.[4]

Why has God arranged this need for diversity to accomplish the Spirit's full purposes? (vv. 24–26)

How does Paul tie all the pieces of this chapter together? (v. 27)

What is clearly the intended answer to the rhetorical questions with which Paul closes his argument? (vv. 29, 30) What is his point?

PAUL'S AD HOC LIST

Two gifts occur in Paul's ad hoc list in verse 28 that will not be covered elsewhere in our study. They're valuable gifts of service which may or may not have been officially recognized positions in the local church. Both would be part of Peter's second broad category: "If anyone ministers, *let him do it* as with the ability which God supplies" (1 Pet. 4:11). (See also under "First . . . Peter" in Lesson 7.)

WORD WEALTH

Helps, *antilempsis.* One with the ability to help or aid someone; a general helper. It occurs only here in the Greek New Testament. A broad based gift, some feel it includes the various activities associated with the gifts of ministry—"he who gives" and "he who shows mercy" (Rom. 12:7, 8).

According to 1 Timothy 5:10, what are some specifics which might be attributed to this gift?

According to Luke 8:3, what is another possible way to demonstrate this gift?

 WORD WEALTH

Administrations, *kubernesis*. Another Greek noun found only here in the New Testament, the word is used in the LXX for giving guidance to someone. Some translate it "giving acts of guidance or wise counsel to the church." It has nothing to do with administrative skills, in spite of the long-standing tradition to translate it "administrations/administrators" in most English Bibles. A cognate noun occurs in Acts 27:11 as "helmsman" and Revelation 18:17 as "shipmaster."

According to Proverbs 1:5, what should characterize someone with this gift?

According to Proverbs 11:14, how does this gift in part operate?

This is a very valuable gift to the church, even if it is mentioned only once. Proverbs makes it clear that wisdom (the ability to judge and act according to God's directives) is a valuable asset; it comes by paying attention to His instruction and living righteously.

AT A GLANCE

Wisdom Cries Out (Prov. 8:1)[5]		
Wisdom is personified in the Proverbs and acts as God's dynamic Word. In the New Testament, Jesus becomes the Wisdom and Word of God.		
Origin of Wisdom	Teaching of Wisdom	Value of Wisdom
In God (v. 22)	Prudence (vv. 5, 12)	Yields riches and honor
From everlasting (v. 23)	Understanding (v. 5)	(v. 18)
Before all things (vv. 23–30)	Excellent things (v. 6)	Greater than gold and
	Truth (v. 7)	silver (v. 19)
	Hatred of wickedness (v. 7)	The wise are blessed
	Righteousness (v. 8)	(vv. 32, 34)
	Knowledge (v. 12)	The wise find life (v. 35)
	Discretion (v. 12)	The foolish love death
	Fear of the Lord (v. 13)	(v. 36)

FAITH ALIVE

What has God said to you personally through this lesson? Do you have an ardent desire to be used in whatever manifestation He may need in a given situation? Are you "praying the price" to be so used?

Are you living in unity with other Christians within the framework of a local congregation? When you gather, do you gather not only with the anticipation of being used in a certain manifestation but with an anticipation to receive from someone else?

Have you ever seen yourself as having the general gift of helps or the specific gift of a counselor? If so, how are you giving yourself to developing and exercising your gift?

Ponder these questions in prayer and then move out in whatever area(s) God's telling you to move. (One word of caution—be sure to walk in full submission to your local church leadership in terms of manifestations of the Spirit in church services. Submission is a vital element behind Holy Spirit fullness.)

1. *Spirit-Filled Life Bible* (Nashville, TN: Thomas Nelson Publishers, 1991), xiv. (combination of #'s 9 and 18.)

2. Ibid., 1516, note on 4:17–21.

3. Gordon Fee, "The First Epistle to the Corinthians," in *The International Commentary on the New Testament* (Grand Rapids, MI: William B. Eerdmans Publishing Co., 1987), 600–601.

4. Ibid., 613.

5. *The Wesley Bible* (Nashville, TN: Thomas Nelson Publishers, 1990), 912, "Chart: Wisdom Cries Out (Prov. 8:1)."

Lesson 11/Word of Wisdom, Word of Knowledge, and Faith

As human beings we love to polarize; as Christians we oftentimes love to do the same. "I believe in predestination. Long live John Calvin!" "I believe in free will. Long live Jacob Arminius!" At times such polarized views have become heated. The initial battle between the Calvinist and Arminian camps became so heated in 1618–19 that a major synod was called in Holland to try to deal with it. Arminianism was condemned, and a leading Arminianist was beheaded a few days after the synod's adjournment. Another Arminianist was imprisoned but escaped.[1]

As has been established in previous lessons, there will always be diversity of interpretation regarding certain biblical matters. Unity does not mean uniformity. But extreme polarization, as exampled above, is rarely if ever fruitful. One area in which this has been true in church history is separating gospel proclamation from gospel demonstration. Jesus obviously both proclaimed and demonstrated the gospel, for Matthew notes that "Jesus went about all Galilee, teaching in their synagogues, preaching the gospel of the kingdom, and healing all kinds of sickness and all kinds of disease among the people" (4:23). His intent was obviously that His church continue in the same wedding, for He told the Twelve, "And as you go, preach . . . heal the sick, cleanse the lepers, raise the dead, cast out demons" (Matt. 10:7, 8).

It is in the demonstration of the proclaimed gospel that the manifestations of the Spirit play a significant role. These manifestations are also vital to bringing believers wholeness beyond justification and to enhancing worship and preaching. Let's delve, then, into their treasure chest, remembering that we are out not only to grow in understanding but to meet the challenge of seeing more demonstrations. We need always to do what we can to "earnestly desire the best gifts" (1 Cor. 12:31).

THE WORD OF WISDOM

It's always somewhat difficult to know exactly how to group the nine manifestations in 1 Corinthians 12:8–10. Our study will simply follow the biblical word. This first gift, "the word of wisdom," together with "the word of knowledge" which follows, is often categorized as aiding in giving instruction. Some term them "the gifts of enlightenment." Using the human mind, these manifestations provide illumination, direction, and spiritual safety.

 WORD WEALTH

Wisdom, *sophia.* Practical wisdom, prudence, skill, comprehensive insight. Christian enlightenment, a right application of knowledge, insight into the true nature of things. Wisdom in the Bible is often coupled with knowledge (Rom. 11:33; 1 Cor. 12:8; Col. 2:3). In anticipation of our needing guidance, direction, and knowing, God tells us to ask for wisdom, assuring us of a liberal reception (James 1:5).[2]

Wisdom in the Bible is a complex matter; at least three different levels are noted.

1) General wisdom—available to all believers to lead normal, godly and stable lives. According to James 1:5–8, how does a Christian get this wisdom?

According to Psalm 119:11, where is the primary place God will direct us to give us this wisdom?

2) Leadership wisdom—available to those who teach, rule, and minister. According to James 3:1, 13, how can we know if a leader is wise?

According to James 1:17, what is the nature of this leadership wisdom?

3) The word of wisdom—a spiritual manifestation available to any believer as a special and specific need might arise. It is supernatural direction which the Holy Spirit Himself shares with an individual for a certain situation, especially where the outcome of decisions would not be known outside this revelation. Its basis is always biblically revealed wisdom.

According to 1 Corinthians 1:8–31, what kind of people is the Spirit likely to use in this manifestation?

According to Ephesians 5:15, 16, what is one reason we need biblical wisdom, including this specific manifestation of the Spirit?

Jesus' statement, "But if I cast out demons by the Spirit of God" (Matt. 12:28), clearly indicates that the Person of the Spirit enabled His ministry. Whereas the evangelists do not directly identify each of the manifestations of the Spirit operating in Jesus' ministry, many are evident. For possible clues as to how the word of wisdom operates, let's look at two incidents in Jesus' life.

1) The request to play a civil judge (Luke 12:13–21)

What is the request?

What is Jesus' "word of wisdom" response?

Jesus' statement in verse 15 seems to establish the root problem with the person involved. What is that problem? What did the possible "word of wisdom" enable Jesus to do in this situation?

2) Jesus' response to paying taxes to Caesar (Matt. 22:15–22)

What is the Pharisees' intent?

According to verse 18, what prompts Jesus' response?

What is the possible "word of wisdom" here?

According to verse 22, what is the effect of this possible gift in His life?

"The 'word of wisdom' is a spiritual utterance at a given moment 'through the Spirit,' supernaturally disclosing the mind, purpose, and way of God as applied to a specific situation."[3]
Further insight into this gift can be learned by studying what it is *not*. Read the following verses in 1 Corinthians and note what "the word of wisdom" is not.

1:17

2:1

2:13

THE WORD OF KNOWLEDGE

WORD WEALTH

Knowledge, gnosis. The recognition of truth by personal experience; a derivative of *ginosko* which means to perceive, understand, recognize, gain knowledge, realize, come to know. *Gnosis* is the knowledge that has an inception, a progress, and an attainment. The precise difference between wisdom and knowledge is not always crystal clear in the Bible. In a general sense, wisdom is the way facts are used or the decisions one makes with information, while knowledge would be the more concrete and specific facts themselves.

According to Acts 5:1–11, how does the word of knowledge appear to be in operation in Peter's life?

The fact that this particular Corinthian gift refers to some sort of special revelation of the Spirit seems to be substantiated by its position between two key revelatory gifts in 1 Corinthians 14:6. What are those gifts?

"Revelation" here implies the revealing of divine "mysteries" (see 1 Cor. 13:2). A biblical "mystery" is a fact or truth which cannot be known apart from the revelation of God to man (cf. 1 Cor. 15:51). Biblical mysteries cannot be discovered by unaided human intellect. "The word of knowledge," then, is a gift of the Spirit giving supernatural insight or information which one would not have known apart from the Spirit's revealing it, such as with Peter and Ananias and Sapphira. It differs from general biblical knowledge in that it's spontaneously revealed rather than learned through study or acquired by experience; however, it must always be tested against revealed biblical knowledge.

What does Daniel 2:27–30 say about the nature of God and the revelation of mysteries in general?

According to John 4:18, how did this gift apparently operate in Jesus' encounter with the Samaritan woman?

According to John 4:19, 28–30, what effect did this possible "word of knowledge" have?

How did Jesus respond to His knowledge of who would betray Him? (John 6:64)

How did this gift apparently operate with reference to Jesus' understanding of Nathanael's home and family background? (John 1:48)

According to 1 Corinthians 8:1, the Corinthians had given the wrong place to *knowledge* (possibly even including this manifestation) in their community. What was their claim?

Contrary to their claim, Paul notes that it is _____ and not knowledge that edifies. How might this serve as a warning to those used in this manifestation?

FAITH

WORD WEALTH

Faith, *pistis*. Conviction, confidence, trust, belief, reliance, trustworthiness, and persuasion. In the New Testament setting, *pistis* is the divinely implanted principle of inward confidence, assurance, trust, and reliance in God and all that He says.[4] It can refer to the body of truth that we believe (1 Tim. 1:19), to the basic trust we have in God for salvation (Eph. 2:8) or to the dynamic power which realizes the energy contained in the promises of God. As a dynamic power, faith is an agency for action; it is this aspect which best describes the 1 Corinthians manifestation. (*Pistis* is also a fruit of the Spirit [Gal. 5:22]. As such it is best translated "faithfulness." See under "Faithfulness" in Lesson 6.)

According to Jeremiah 32:17, at the root of this gift is an ability to confess what with confidence?

Mark 9:14–29 gives us some insight into the power of such a manifestation of faith. Read the account and answer the following:

What is going on here?

According to verses 17, 18, what is Jesus "up against"?

Judging from Jesus' response in verse 19, what seemingly indicates that His action is indeed a manifestation of faith?

According to verse 22, what is the father's concern?

How does Jesus respond to the father's "if You can do anything . . ."? (v. 23)

How does Jesus demonstrate faith in this particular instance? (v. 25)

What is apparently often linked to the manifestation of faith? (v. 29)

According to Acts 3:4–6, this manifestation apparently prompted Peter to do what?

What resulted? (vv. 7–10)

To what did Peter attribute the healing? (v. 16)

Most scholars believe this manifestation operated in certain Old Testament saints even though the incidents are not specified as manifestations of the Spirit. They are simply termed acts of faith. This being the case, let's explore!

According to Hebrews 11:32–34, what might we expect to result from this manifestation?

Read 1 Kings 18:20–40. What is Elijah's challenge? (vv. 20–24)

According to verse 27, Elijah had such confidence in God that he _____ his opponents.

According to verses 33–35, his God-inspired confidence prompted him to do what?

What resulted? (vv. 38–40)

 PROBING THE DEPTHS

Carefully read Mark 11:20–26 and note the following:

What kind of "heart" is necessary to exercise this gift? (v. 23)

In addition to an inner assurance, this gift calls for us to do what? (v. 23)

What is linked with this gift of faith? (v. 24)

What other important element is involved in demonstrating this gift? (vv. 25, 26)

Using two or three scholarly commentaries, study the implications of Jesus' phrase, "Have faith in God" (v. 22).

The manifestation of *faith* is the spontaneously granted spiritual ability to release the energy of God for any given action or need; it is to be differentiated from faith that leads to salvation or from general Christian faith developed through a daily walk with the Spirit. Scholars often term this manifestation, along with *gifts of healings* and *the working of miracles*, as "the gifts of energy" or "the gifts of ministry."

 AT A GLANCE

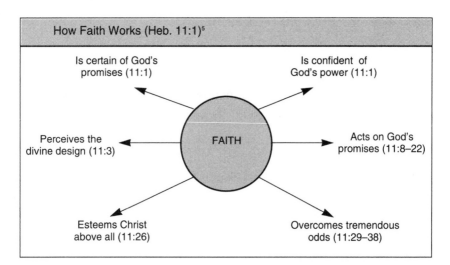

How Faith Works (Heb. 11:1)[5]

Is certain of God's promises (11:1)

Is confident of God's power (11:1)

Perceives the divine design (11:3)

FAITH

Acts on God's promises (11:8–22)

Esteems Christ above all (11:26)

Overcomes tremendous odds (11:29–38)

 **FAITH ALIVE**

We've now examined three of the nine gifts. Can you identify areas in your life or ministry which could substantially benefit from God's using you in any or all of these? When you gather corporately, assuming it is acceptable to the leadership in charge, do you worship anticipating God to make such revelations to you or to use you in a demonstration faith? Are

your earnestly seeking these gifts? Ponder these questions
and take them to God in prayer, remembering that our intent
is to both grow in knowledge and experience.

1. Kenneth Scott Latourette, *A History of Christianity, Vol. II* (San Francisco, CA:
Harper & Row, Publishers, 1975), 765.
2. *Spirit-Filled Life Bible* (Nashville, TN: Thomas Nelson Publishers, 1991), 1636,
"Word Wealth: 6:10 wisdom."
3. Ibid., 1736, note on 12:8–11.
4. Ibid., 1492, "Word Wealth: 11:22 faith."
5. *The Wesley Bible* (Nashville, TN: Thomas Nelson Publishers, 1990), 1858, "Chart:
How Faith Works (Heb. 11:1)."

Lesson 12/Gifts of Healings, the Working of Miracles, and Prophecy

It is probably quite safe to say that these gifts are among the most challenging of the nine—especially gifts of healings and miracles. It seems that if these manifestations are evident in the church at all, it's always "over there"—in Africa or India or someplace else where YOU aren't! Their operation in the church today also challenges the skepticism in all of us, for the truth of the matter is, when they do happen "over there," it's hard to document them. Some leading opponents of these manifestations in the church today say the answer to that one is simple. They're hard to document because they aren't happening. You can't document what isn't there!

And then there are those who do believe they happen, even over here, who have had to face a loved one's death from a terminal disease or the loss of a job or house or even relationship because "the healing" or "miracle" never came through. A cross-country trip to the "faith healer" didn't even work, let alone the seemingly endless intercession and faith of the local saints.

And what about prophecy? Of course, there have been numerous prophetic words that many of us may have heard that have focused, encouraged, and stabilized us. But also, many have heard "prophetic promises" of blessing, prosperity and revival that have never come to pass, at least apparently not as yet—or not as the "prophecy" suggested.

What's a sincere Christian to do? What's he/she to do? Keep pressing on, that's what. We don't want to overwork a single principle, but in this entire matter of spiritual manifestations we MUST remember 1 Corinthians 13:9, 12: "For we know in part and we prophesy in part . . . for now we see in a mirror, dimly." We lived trapped between the present, in-part blessings of the kingdom of God and the yet-future, consummated blessings. The Spirit and His manifestations are as available today as in the first century, but that doesn't mean we can pull consummated perfection into our experience if we just do or believe the right things. This was not even the case in the early church. The same Paul who stretched himself over the lifeless body of Eutychus and saw a miraculous resuscitation (Acts 20:9, 10), told Timothy, "Trophimus I have left in Miletus sick" (2 Tim. 4:20) without the slightest intimation it was because of a lack of faith or any other such thing. It was likely the result of the fact that the consummated kingdom is not here and, for reasons we do not understand, God sovereignly chose not to touch Trophimus. As we contend for these gifts, we must not overlook the element of sovereignty, for Paul clearly says, "One and the same Spirit works all these things, distributing to each one individually as He wills" (1 Cor. 12:11). Why a release of healing or any other manifestation to one person and not to another? Only God knows. Our responsibility is to "earnestly desire"; His is to distribute.

GIFTS OF HEALINGS

What this gift is all about really needs little comment; the physical body is important to God (1 Thess. 5:23) and needs His healing touch on occasion. The origin of the early church's expectation of miraculous physical healing is the ministry of Jesus Himself, a ministry anchored in the Old Testament. "He [Jesus] cast out the spirits with a word, and healed all who were sick, that it might be fulfilled which was spoken by Isaiah the prophet . . ." (Matt. 8:16, 17). "Only among the intellectuals and in a 'scientific age' is it thought to be too hard for

God to heal the sick . . . this is also unfortunately true of many contemporary Christians, whose theology has made a severe disjunction between the 'then' and 'now' of God's working. This seems to be a seriously flawed understanding of the kingdom, which according to the NT was inaugurated by Christ in the power of the Spirit, who continues the work of the kingdom until the consummation."[1]

Read the following scriptures, noting with whom/what sickness is often associated.

Luke 13:16

John 5:13, 14

James 5:15

Read the following scriptures, noting God's will with regard to healing.

Ex. 15:25b, 26

Ex. 23:25

Ps. 103:1–3

According to 1 Corinthians 6:13, what is God's view of the human body?

God emphatically puts Himself on the side of healing and has put a healing impulse in man to fight against disease and sickness. There are a number of reasons given in the Bible why people aren't healed, including a lack of faith and possible sin in their lives; the number one reason, however, why people are not healed is that noted above—*the kingdom is not yet consummated in terms of experiencing healing,* even though Jesus made perfect provision for healing with His work on the Cross. There is nothing we can do to experience the consummated kingdom prior to Jesus' return except to praise God for the day when all sickness is *experientially* put under His feet! But in all this, God has only one will—He wants humankind healed. He Himself no doubt feels the grief of His self-imposed limits with reference to kingdom manifestations now. When people aren't healed, it has nothing to do with God's will; it has to do with the fact that the fullness of what Jesus purchased yet awaits His return to be totally and conclusively activated. Flashes of kingdom fullness do appear on occasion, and we never know when the gifts of healings will be released. We should then always pray and anticipate a manifestation of the gifts of healings, knowing God wants to heal.

JESUS AND HEALINGS

How does Matthew in part summarize Jesus' ministry? (4:23; 9:35)

How does Luke summarize it? (Acts 10:38)

Matthew applies Isaiah 53:4 to Jesus' physical healing ministry (8:16, 17). To what does Peter apply this same verse? (1 Pet. 2:24) What does this tell us about the prophecy from Isaiah?

According to Romans 8:9–11, what does the Holy Spirit want to give to our bodies?

The context here shows that the life the Spirit gives includes our ultimate physical resurrection; however, the following appeal (vv. 12–18) shows that it also refers to giving life here and now through physical healing.

WHY GIFTS OF HEALINGS?

Paul consistently uses the plural with both "gift" and "healing" (1 Cor. 12:9, 28, 30). No one knows for sure why this is. Some scholars feel "gifts" is plural to reinforce the fact that this manifestation is not a permanent, residing gift. As with all the manifestations, it is available to any member of the body as the Spirit wills; even if one manifests this gift repeatedly, he/she does not own it and should probably never use it as a title, that is, "Faith Healer Robert Smith."

As to why "healings" is plural, perhaps we have a clue from the medical world where we learn that healing is a vast subject. It is not uncommon for a medical doctor to specialize in a given area of medicine. Furthermore, humankind can be sick physically, emotionally, mentally and spiritually. The plural *may* indicate, then, that the Holy Spirit uses certain individuals more specifically for some disorders and other individuals for other disorders. (Such fits the context of mutual interdependence and would certainly help prevent those used in this tremendous manifestation from having it "go to their heads.") The plurals here *may* also indicate the variety of ways in which this manifestation is released.

Read the following and note the various ways in which Jesus healed:

Matt. 8:1–4

Matt. 8:5–13

Matt. 9:18–26

Mark 7:31–37

John 9:6, 7

THE WORKING OF MIRACLES

 WORD WEALTH

Miracle, *dunamis.* One of four Greek words for "power," *dunamis* is also one of three Greek words used to describe supernatural events. *Semeia* (signs) and *terata* (wonders) are the other two (see Acts 2:22). *Dunamis* means energy, power, might, great force, great ability, strength, or miracle. When translated "miracle," it describes the power of the age to come at work upon the Earth beyond the ordinary course of natural law. (Compare "dynamic" and "dynamite.")

According to Mark 9:1, what accompanies the presence of the kingdom?

According to Mark 5:30, the healing of the woman with the issue of blood was a release of _____.

Each of the following texts uses *dunamis* to describe a supernatural event. Read them and note what the New Testament calls a "miracle."

Luke 1:34, 35

Luke 4:36

Luke 9:1

Acts 19:11, 12

According to Luke 10:19, God's church needs the working of miracles to counter what?

According to Matthew 11:20–24, the working of miracles has a purpose even beyond the specific good it accomplishes. What is that purpose?

According to Matthew 13:54, Jesus' life reflected both the working of miracles and _____.

According to John 14:12–14, why is it reasonable for Christians to expect this manifestation?

According to Acts 1:8, the coming of the Holy Spirit brings _____. What is to be the result of this?

According to Acts 5:15 and 9:40, what are some ways Acts 1:8 was fulfilled in Peter's life?

The manifestation of the working of miracles, then, is God working to do what could not be done naturally. The working of miracles transcends the natural laws of the Earth; they are a result of Holy Spirit fullness in the life of earnestly seeking believers as they display power flowing out from the Spirit within (cf. Luke 4:14). This gift is broad based and diverse, as seen above. "Although Paul would probably include gifts of healings under 'the working of miracles,' this manifestation most likely covers all other kinds of supernatural activities beyond the healing of the sick."[2]

PROPHECY

We have previously established that "prophecy" is a very broad based biblical concept. Before proceeding, therefore, you need to take a moment to review "Prophecy" under Lesson 8 and "Some Prophets" under Lesson 9.

In order to clearly understand this manifestation, we need to recall Peter's sermon on the Day of Pentecost (Acts 2:14–36). "According to Acts 2:4, 4:31 all are filled with the prophetic Spirit and according to Acts 2:16ff it is a specific mark of the age of fulfillment that the Spirit does not only lay hold of individuals but that all members of the eschatological community with distinction are called to prophesy."[3] This manifestation of the Spirit, then, "consisted of spontaneous, Spirit-inspired, intelligible messages, orally delivered in the gathered assembly, intended for the edification or encouragement of the people. Thus it is *not* the delivery of a previously prepared sermon . . . the implication of 14:24 is that it is a gift available—at least potentially—to all."[4]

1 CORINTHIANS 14

We learn a great deal about the operation and purpose of this manifestation from Paul's contrast of it in 1 Corinthians 14 with the "*different* kinds of tongues" and "the interpretation of tongues" in 1 Corinthians 12.

What is Paul's exhortation regarding prophecy? (v. 1)

What are three primary purposes of prophecy? (v. 3)

Who benefits from prophetic words? (v. 4)

Why is it that "he who prophesies is greater than he who speaks with tongues"? (v. 5)

Why does Paul prefer prophecy in congregational meetings? (v. 19)

According to verse 22, prophecy is *primarily* for whom?

According to verses 24 and 25, prophecy does have a role in the life of the *uninformed* or *unbelievers*. What is that role?

"Uninformed" (Greek, *idiotes*) refers to someone who's untutored in something; in this case it's Christianity. They are likely, therefore, unbelievers, although some see them as believers who are uninformed in matters of spiritual manifestations.

What synonym does Paul use for "prophecy" in verse 26?

According to verse 29, all prophetic utterances must be _____.

"Two or three" is not Paul's way of saying that a maximum of three legitimate prophecies can be given in any one congregational meeting. This would contradict his instruction that "all" can potentially prophesy (vv. 24, 31). His contextual concern is that there should be no more than three prophetic words at a time before "the others judge." To judge a prophecy is to discern its conformation to established biblical truth *and* its relevancy or applicability to the meeting at hand. Prophetic words can be doctrinally correct, yet out of place, because they're ill timed or they are words to the individual rather than the entire group. In this case, they are best held and pondered by the individual, remembering that "the spirits of the prophets are subject to the prophets" (v. 32), and "if *anything* is revealed to another who sits by, let the first keep silent" (v. 30).

According to verse 31, what is another function of prophecy?

What do we learn in verse 32 about "prophetic control"?

WORD WEALTH

Subject, *hupotasso.* Literally "to stand under." The word suggests subordination, obedience, submission, subservience, subjection. The divine gift of prophetic utterance is put under the control and responsibility of the possessor.[5]

"Prophecy" may overlap at times with "the word of wisdom" or "the word of knowledge" when giving practical direction to situations; prophecy, however, seems primarily directed to the congregation as a whole, while the other two manifestations are more to individuals. This manifestation basically does in specific situations and through varied believers what the Ephesians 4:11 office prophet does on a more ongoing basis.

PROBING THE DEPTHS

There is considerable debate as to whether or not this gift should be given with a "Thus says the Lord God" attached. Using a concordance, look up at least a dozen times in which this particular phrase is used in the Bible. Who uses it? Are there any NT prophecies given using this nomenclature? What conclusion(s) can we draw? Do you personally think the 1 Corinthians 12 manifestation of prophecy should be given using, "Thus says the Lord God"? Why or why not? If yes, should a distinction be drawn between its use now and its use with the OT classical prophets? If so, what? Avoid a dogmatic attitude, but draw a practical conclusion.

1. Gordon D. Fee, "The First Epistle to the Corinthians," in *The International Commentary on the New Testament* (Grand Rapids, MI: William B. Eerdmans Publishing Co., 1987), 594.

2. Ibid.

3. Gerhard Friedrich, *Theological Dictionary of the New Testament*, Vol. VI, eds. Gerhard Kittel and Gerhard Friedrich (Grand Rapids, MI: William B. Eerdmans Publishing Co., 1975), 849.

4. Fee, "The First Epistle to the Corinthians," 595–596.

5. *Spirit-Filled Life Bible* (Nashville, TN: Thomas Nelson Publishers, 1991), 1742, "Word Wealth: 14:22 subject."

Lesson 13/Discerning of Spirits, Different Kinds of Tongues, and the Interpretation of Tongues

We have arrived at the final three manifestations of the Spirit in 1 Corinthians 12! Hopefully it has been a rewarding and encouraging pursuit so far, a pursuit that has indeed further encouraged you to "earnestly desire the best gifts." We noted in Lesson 10 that it is difficult to know exactly how to categorize these nine manifestations. Assuming our ad hoc classification under "Being More Fully Informed" (Lesson 10) is correct, the purposes of the manifestations in this lesson have to do with more effectively ministering to people's needs ("discerning of spirits") and more effectively worshiping God ("*different* kinds of tongues"; "the interpretation of tongues").

If you have any experience at all in dealing with people, especially those who've had affiliation with the occult, you know there are spirit beings beyond God. Aware of the fact that the source of evil is often difficult to discern, God has given the manifestation of "discerning of spirits" to help us "see" behind the scenes of the spirit realm.

It appears that of all the manifestations, the gifts of "*different* kinds of tongues" and "the interpretation of tongues" were causing the most confusion in Corinth. They may have even been among the most controversial in the congregation.

Some two thousand years has hardly changed matters, which is unfortunate, for as Jack W. Hayford has observed, the sensitive, scriptural exercising of these gifts has the potential to accomplish a great work.[1] Let's plunge into our final study together and see more fully what these three manifestations are all about.

DISCERNING OF SPIRITS

The Greek word translated "discerning" *(diakrisis)* is the cognate of the verb translated "judge" in 1 Corinthians 14:29. It has to do with differentiating or properly judging "spirits." Scholars disagree as to what Paul means by "spirits." The most common consensus is that it refers to the various spirits of the vast spiritual realm. Hence, "discerning of spirits" has to do with properly judging what is of the Spirit of God and what is of other spirits. It is a divine aid in fulfilling the command of 1 John 4:1, "Beloved, do not believe every spirit, but test the spirits, whether they are of God."

DEFINING SPIRITS

Read the following and note who the Bible deems "spirit beings."

Mark 1:27

John 4:24

Rom. 8:16

Eph. 2:2

Heb. 1:13, 14

WHY THIS GIFT?

According to 2 Corinthians 11:12–15, what is one reason the church needs the gift of discerning of spirits?

According to 2 Thessalonians 2:9, 10, what are some ways Satan transforms himself to practice deception?

According to Matthew 24:3, 11, what is one reason Jesus gives for our needing this manifestation?

What is one way in which this gift might operate in helping judge prophetic words? (1 Cor. 14:29)

There is obviously a vast difference between God and Satan, angels and demons. We do not live in a spiritual vacuum, so we need discernment to know the origin of given manifestations. People can be filled with the Spirit of God or they can be demonized. Furthermore, "symptoms" can sometimes be misleading, as noted in the opening example from the ministry of Judith MacNutt. (How many times have you known two Christians to disagree over the source of bondage in a person's life?—"It's flesh!" "No, it's demons!") The matter of evil is not simple. To insure the safety of believers and to be able to know the source and the value of things happening in the spiritual realm, the Holy Spirit gives this manifestation.

Because "spirits" is somewhat ambiguous, this manifestation may also allow for a certain sensitivity to the nature or state of the human spirit itself. Read the following and note a couple of possible states of the human spirit.

Prov. 18:14

Is. 57:15

"**Discerning of spirits** is the ability to discern the spirit world, and especially to detect the true source of circumstances or motives of people."[2]

In an unpublished manuscript Jack W. Hayford has written, "In the exercise of the gift of discernment, we are dealing with an insight into the invisible—with an ability to 'divide between' the human and the hellish (the flesh and the devil) and often with the ability to determine the source or root of a problem as it stems from the spiritual realm."

JESUS AND THE DISCERNING OF SPIRITS

In terms of frequency of occurrence, the number one recorded miracle of Jesus' ministry is that of exorcisms. This flowed from His tremendous sensitivity to the unseen realm.

Read Mark 1:21–28 carefully.

What did the man in the synagogue do? (vv. 23, 24)

To what is his behavior attributed? (v. 23)

How did Jesus respond? (v. 25)

How did the demon respond? (v. 26)

What effect did this have on the people? (v. 27)

According to Mark 2:6–8, how did the "discerning of spirits" apparently operate on occasion in Jesus' life?

Read Luke 13:10–17. Although it is not directly attributed to this manifestation, what valuable insight *likely* resulted from this gift in operation regarding the source of the woman's ailment? (vv. 11, 16)

"*DIFFERENT* KINDS OF TONGUES" AND "THE INTERPRETATION OF TONGUES"

Although the gift of tongues (Greek, *glossa*) has value apart from being interpreted (see below), these two are virtually companion gifts. We will therefore examine them together, after which we'll look at the uniqueness of tongues alone.

We cannot be certain whether or not Paul understood the manifestation of "*different* kinds of tongues" to be actual human languages or "the tongues . . . of angels" referenced in 1 Corinthians 13:1. Known languages spoken supernaturally is clearly what happened in Acts 2:4–13, where Luke uses *glossa* to describe the phenomenon at Pentecost. "*Different* kinds of tongues is the gift of speaking supernaturally in a language not known to the individual. The plural allows different forms, possibly harmonizing the known spoken languages of Acts 2:4–6 and the unknown transrational utterances in Corinthians, designed particularly for praying and singing in the Spirit, mostly for private worship (14:14–19)."[3] In some regards the issue is irrelevant; Paul's main point is that what is spoken is unknown to both the speaker and hearer and needs the companion gift of interpretation to benefit the gathered assembly.

As with the manifestation of prophecy (see Lesson 12), the manifestations of "*different* kinds of tongues" and "the interpretation of tongues" receive considerable space in 1 Corinthians 14. Paul's purpose is to give detailed understanding and regulation to the matter of tongues, apparently because they were out of control at Corinth. Let's examine the chapter, therefore, to see what we can learn.

To whom are tongues addressed? (v. 2)

What is one uttering when speaking in tongues? (v. 2)

"Mysteries" here likely has a specialized New Testament meaning of sounds which both speaker and hearer do not understand. These mysteries are spoken to God; the person is communing with God by praying or worshiping in the will of God through the use of supernatural language inspired by the Holy Spirit (cf. v. 15).

      Who primarily benefits from the manifestation of tongues? (v. 4)

      What is Paul's desire relative to Christians' speaking in tongues? (v. 5)

      When "*different* kinds of tongues" are interpreted, what is the effect on the congregation? (v. 5)

      Jack Hayford has noted that, according to 1 Corinthians 14:5, an interpreted "tongue" has value and purpose just as does the prophetic word."[4] It is likely because of this truth that so many interpreted tongues are churchward, while "private" or "devoted" tongues are only addressed to God.

      Because an uninterpreted tongue does not profit the hearers (cf. 12:7), what is Paul's exhortation in verse 13?

      The interpretation of tongues may be given by a person other than the one speaking in tongues (12:11), but the burden for the interpretation must rest with the one who speaks in tongues. Although the Greek word for "interpretation" *(hermeneia)* can mean "translation," it also means "to put into words." Here, therefore, it likely means to put the content of the tongue into words which the congregation understands, as opposed to giving a literal translation.

According to verse 14, what is involved when we "pray in a tongue"?

Knowing the value of this manifestation, what is Paul's resolve? (v. 15)

According to verse 16, what are two other purposes of this manifestation?

With reference to unbelievers present in congregational meetings, tongues must be exercised with order or what is likely to happen? (vv. 22, 23)

According to verse 27, what is one way to bring regulatory order to tongues?

It is not clear whether *"let there be* two or at the most three" refers to the maximum number of times this manifestation is to be exercised in a given meeting or to the maximum number of tongues before there is an interpretation. (See under "1 Corinthians 14" in Lesson 12 for Paul's numerical regulation of prophecy.) In favor of the former is Paul's "at the most," a limitation missing from his prophetic control instruction. At any rate, *"each* in turn" clearly covers his main point: "Let all things be done for edification" (v. 26).

According to verse 28, if one is not certain he or someone else present will be used to interpret, what is he to do?

According to verse 28, does this mean one should not pray "quietly" in tongues in corporate settings?

THE UNIQUENESS OF TONGUES

Perhaps you have noticed a couple of aspects of tongues that are different from the general aspects of the 1 Corinthians 12 manifestations. 1) "He who speaks in a tongue edifies himself" (1 Cor. 14:4) is in contrast to 12:7, "The manifestation of the Spirit is given to each one for the profit *of all."* "The profit *of all"* comes only with the companion gift of interpretation (14:5). 2) "I wish you all spoke with tongues" (14:5) and "I will pray with the spirit" (14:15) stand in contrast to 12:11, "But one and the same Spirit works all these things, distributing to each one individually as He wills." From this evidence, it seems quite clear that the gift of tongues is of two varieties—the corporate manifestation of 1 Corinthians 12:10 which comes under the regulations of 12:11 and 14:1–33— *and* a gift for private, personalized prayer and worship. This latter gift can be exercised at any time, even publicly without interpretation, so long as the person speaks quietly and privately "to himself and to God" (14:28). This latter use is undoubtedly tongues' foremost purpose (14:14–18), for "in the church I would rather speak five words with my understanding, that I may teach others also, than ten thousand words in a tongue" (14:19).

 FAITH ALIVE

What is your attitude toward the manifestation of "*different* kinds of tongues"? If you favor this manifestation and practice it, either privately and/or corporately, how is your attitude toward those who do not? What about toward those who even despise it and/or do not feel it is for today? If you're not sure about this manifestation today, how open are you to a fresh look at the biblical evidence? Is "tradition" perhaps governing you more than the Bible? Consider these matters in prayer, giving great diligence to your attitude and to any growth God might want to bring you.

CONCLUSION

Hopefully, this has been a prosperous journey, or should we say, the beginning of a journey. The Spirit-filled life, including the growth of His fruit and manifestations, is a daily, ongoing pursuit, as Paul reminds us in Ephesians 5:18. Though in your experience and theology Spirit fullness may have a definite starting point, may it never have an ending point this side of heaven! May you seek His face in diligent, fervent prayer for the proper attitude and availability to be the salt and light Jesus needs in a hurting, sin-controlled world. May your life-long ambition be to obey 1 Corinthians 14:1: "Pursue love, and desire spiritual *gifts*."

1. Jack W. Hayford, "Tongues and Interpretation," *Charisma*, November 1992, Lake Mary, FL, 63–64.

2. *Spirit-Filled Life Bible* (Nashville, TN: Thomas Nelson Publishers, 1991), 1737, note on 12:8–11.

3. Ibid.

4. Jack W. Hayford, "Tongues and Interpretaion," 64.